Learning Linux Shell Scripting
Second Edition

Leverage the power of shell scripts to solve real-world problems

Ganesh Naik

BIRMINGHAM - MUMBAI

Learning Linux Shell Scripting
Second Edition

Commissioning Editor: Gebin George
Acquisition Editor: Shrilekha Inani
Content Development Editor: Priyanka Deshpande
Technical Editor: Prashant Chaudhari
Copy Editor: Safis Editing
Project Coordinator: Virginia Dias
Proofreader: Safis Editing
Indexer: Aishwarya Gangawane
Graphics: Tom Scaria
Production Coordinator: Nilesh Mohite

First published: December 2015
Second edition: May 2018

Production reference: 1150518

Published by Packt Publishing Ltd.
Livery Place
35 Livery Street
Birmingham
B3 2PB, UK.

ISBN 978-1-78899-319-7

www.packtpub.com

I wish to dedicate this book to my Gurudev, His Holiness Dr. Jayant Balaji Athavale. I wish to express gratitude for his guidance, which I have received on how to become good human being, good professional, and a seeker on the path of spiritual progress.
- Ganesh Sanjiv Naik

`mapt.io`

Mapt is an online digital library that gives you full access to over 5,000 books and videos, as well as industry leading tools to help you plan your personal development and advance your career. For more information, please visit our website.

Why subscribe?

- Spend less time learning and more time coding with practical eBooks and Videos from over 4,000 industry professionals

- Improve your learning with Skill Plans built especially for you

- Get a free eBook or video every month

- Mapt is fully searchable

- Copy and paste, print, and bookmark content

PacktPub.com

Did you know that Packt offers eBook versions of every book published, with PDF and ePub files available? You can upgrade to the eBook version at `www.PacktPub.com` and as a print book customer, you are entitled to a discount on the eBook copy. Get in touch with us at `service@packtpub.com` for more details.

At `www.PacktPub.com`, you can also read a collection of free technical articles, sign up for a range of free newsletters, and receive exclusive discounts and offers on Packt books and eBooks.

Contributors

About the author

Ganesh Naik is an author, consultant, and corporate trainer for embedded Android, embedded Linux, IoT, and machine learning related product development. He has more than 20 years, professional experience and project accomplishment in information technology. He has worked as a corporate trainer for the Indian Space Research Organization, Intel, GE, Samsung, Motorola, Penang Skills Development Center, and various companies in Singapore and India. He has started a company called Levana Technologies, which works with organizations for consulting and training activities.

I would like to thank my wife, Vishalakshi, for providing valuable suggestions, support, and continuous motivation. Also, my colleague, Mansi Joshi, who provided feedback from a technical perspective.

A big thanks to the entire team at Packt: Shrilekha Inani, Priyanka Deshpande, and Prashant Chaudhari, for providing me with very positive and motivating support throughout the book.

About the reviewer

Shawn Soloman is a technology veteran with a wide range of skill sets from 20+ years in the technology field. While working in the ISP, VoIP, educational, open source development and disaster recovery fields, his skill set has adapted and broadened over the years.

Packt is searching for authors like you

If you're interested in becoming an author for Packt, please visit `authors.packtpub.com` and apply today. We have worked with thousands of developers and tech professionals, just like you, to help them share their insight with the global tech community. You can make a general application, apply for a specific hot topic that we are recruiting an author for, or submit your own idea.

Table of Contents

Preface

Shell scripts are an essential part of any modern operating system, such as Unix, Linux, or Windows. The scripting language and its syntax may vary from OS to OS, but the fundamental principles remain the same. I first encountered Linux shell scripts during the development of embedded Linux product development. Shell scripts initialized the complete product, from basic booting procedure to the user logging, to the complete operating system being initialized. Another situation was automation of regular activities such as build and release management of the source codes of very complex products, where more than 10,000 files were part of the single project. Similarly, another very common requirement is, automatic routine administration activities.

Initially, I learned scripts to solve practical problems and customize pre-existing products. This book is a summary of what I have learned over the years about Linux shell scripting through project development work, consultancy, and corporate training and Q&A sessions.

In this book, we will learn the very basics of shell scripting to real-world complex, customized automation. By the end of the book, the reader will be able to confidently use their own shell scripts for the real-world problems out there. The idea is to be as practical as possible and give the reader the look and feel of what real-world scripting looks like.

This book covers the GNU Bourne Again Shell (BASH) scripting. You can use the knowledge gained by reading this book for any shell of any of the UNIX flavors or Linux distributions. You may need to take care of few syntax changes if you are working in other shells, such as Korn or similar. You should be able to read this book cover to cover, or just pick it up and read anything you find interesting. But, perhaps most importantly, if you have a question about how to solve a particular problem or you need a hint, you will find it easy to find the right solution—or something close enough—to save your time and energy.

Who this book is for

This book is for readers who are proficient at working with Linux and who want to learn about shell scripting to improve their efficiency and practical skills. The following are few examples where we can use the skills we learned in this book:

- Shell scripting for automating tasks such as taking periodic backup
- System administration
- Database maintenance and backup
- Test processing and report generation
- Customization of system initialization
- Embedded Linux product developments

What this book covers

Chapter 1, *Getting Started and Working with Shell Scripting*, introduces different ways to write and run shell scripts. We'll also learn ways to handle files and directories, as well as working with permissions.

Chapter 2, *Drilling Deep into Process Management, Job Control, and Automation*, speaks about basic process management. We will learn about command ps and also about job management using commands such as jobs, fg, bg, kill, and pkill. Later on, we will learn about process monitoring tools top, iostat, vmstat, and sar.

Chapter 3, *Using Text Processing and Filters in Your Scripts*, speaks about using more, less, head, and tail commands. We will also learn about text processing tools such as cut, paste, comm, and uniq. We will learn what is a standard input, output, and standard error. Later on, we will learn about meta-characters and pattern matching using VI and grep.

Chapter 4, *Working with Commands*, explains how shell interprets any command entered on the command line. We will also learn about command substitution, separators, and pipes in detail.

Chapter 5, *Exploring Expressions and Variables*, speaks about variables in general and environment variables in particular. This includes how to export environment variables, set, shift, read-only variables, command-line arguments, and create and handle arrays.

Chapter 6, *Neat Tricks with Shell Scripting*, talks about debugging, here operator, and interactive shell scripts for taking input from keyboard and file handling.

Chapter 7, *Performing Arithmetic Operations in Shell Scripts*, covers performing arithmetic operations in various ways such as using declare, let, expr, and arithmetic expressions. We will also learn about representing numbers in different bases such as hex, octal, and binary. The chapter also covers using bc utility for performing floating point or fractional arithmetic.

Chapter 8, *Automating Decision Making in Scripts*, talks about using decision making in scripts by working with Test, if-else, and switching case. We will also learn about how to use select with for loop along with the menu.

Chapter 9, *Automating Repetitive Tasks*, speaks about repeating tasks such as doing routine administration activities using the for loop, while loop, and do while loop. We will also learn how control loops using break statement and continue statement.

Chapter 10, *Working with Functions*, speaks about functions in shell scripts. We will learn how to define and display functions, and further how to remove the function from the shell. We will also learn about passing arguments to functions, sharing data between functions, declaring local variables in a function, returning result from a function, and running functions in the background. We will finally learn about using source and .(dot) commands. We will use these commands for using the library of functions.

Chapter 11, *Using Advanced Functionality in Scripts*, covers using traps and signals. We will also learn about creating menus with the help of dialog utility.

Chapter 12, *System Start-up and Customizing a Linux System*, speaks about the Linux system start-up, from power on until user login and how to customize a Linux system environment.

Chapter 13, *Pattern Matching and Regular Expressions with sed and awk*, talks about regular expressions and using sed (stream editor) and awk for text processing. We will learn how to use various commands and options along with a lot of examples for using sed and awk.

Chapter 14, *Taking Backup and Embedding Other Languages in Shell Scripts*, speaks about taking backup locally as well as across the network. We will also learn about automating it using crontab. We will learn about embedding other languages in bash scripts such as Python, Ruby, and Pearl.

Chapter 15, *Database Administration Using Shell Scripts*, talks about how to write and execute MySQL commands in a shell script as well as how to write and execute Oracle commands in a shell script. By using learnings from this chapter, we will be able to automate frequently required database administration tasks.

To get the most out of this book

Any computer that has Linux OS installed in it will be sufficient for learning all the topics discussed in this book. For the first edition, we used Ubuntu Linux distribution. For this second edition, we have used CentOS Linux distribution. I have personally tested all the commands and scripts in Ubuntu 16.04, as well as in the CentOS 7.0 distribution.

During the course, if you find that any particular utility is not installed in Ubuntu or any Debian-based distribution, then enter the following command to install that utility:

```
$ sudo apt-get update
$ sudo apt-get install package-name
```

A good internet connection should be available for the preceding commands to run.

In CentOS or any other rpm-based distribution, enter the following commands:

```
$ sudo yum update
$ sudo yum install package-name
```

If the internet is connected, then using these commands you can install any command or utility that is not already installed.

Download the example code files

You can download the example code files for this book from your account at www.packtpub.com. If you purchased this book elsewhere, you can visit www.packtpub.com/support and register to have the files emailed directly to you.

You can download the code files by following these steps:

1. Log in or register at www.packtpub.com.
2. Select the **SUPPORT** tab.
3. Click on **Code Downloads & Errata**.
4. Enter the name of the book in the **Search** box and follow the onscreen instructions.

Once the file is downloaded, please make sure that you unzip or extract the folder using the latest version of:

- WinRAR/7-Zip for Windows
- Zipeg/iZip/UnRarX for Mac
- 7-Zip/PeaZip for Linux

The code bundle for the book is also hosted on GitHub at `https://github.com/PacktPublishing/Learning-Linux-Shell-Scripting-Second-Edition`. In case there's an update to the code, it will be updated on the existing GitHub repository.

We also have other code bundles from our rich catalogue of books and videos available at `https://github.com/PacktPublishing/`. Check them out!

Conventions used

There are a number of text conventions used throughout this book.

`CodeInText`: Indicates code words in text, database table names, folder names, filenames, file extensions, pathnames, dummy URLs, user input, and Twitter handles. Here is an example: "Mount the downloaded `WebStorm-10*.dmg` disk image file as another disk in your system."

A block of code is set as follows:

```
#!/bin/bash
# This is comment line
echo "Hello World"
ls
date
```

When we wish to draw your attention to a particular part of a code block, the relevant lines or items are set in bold:

```
#!/bin/bash
# This is comment line
echo "Hello World"
ls
date
```

Any command-line input or output is written as follows:

```
$ bash hello.sh
```

Bold: Indicates a new term, an important word, or words that you see onscreen. For example, words in menus or dialog boxes appear in the text like this. Here is an example: "Select **System info** from the **Administration** panel."

Warnings or important notes appear like this.

Tips and tricks appear like this.

Get in touch

Feedback from our readers is always welcome.

General feedback: Email `feedback@packtpub.com` and mention the book title in the subject of your message. If you have questions about any aspect of this book, please email us at `questions@packtpub.com`.

Errata: Although we have taken every care to ensure the accuracy of our content, mistakes do happen. If you have found a mistake in this book, we would be grateful if you would report this to us. Please visit `www.packtpub.com/submit-errata`, selecting your book, clicking on the Errata Submission Form link, and entering the details.

Piracy: If you come across any illegal copies of our works in any form on the Internet, we would be grateful if you would provide us with the location address or website name. Please contact us at `copyright@packtpub.com` with a link to the material.

If you are interested in becoming an author: If there is a topic that you have expertise in and you are interested in either writing or contributing to a book, please visit `authors.packtpub.com`.

Reviews

Please leave a review. Once you have read and used this book, why not leave a review on the site that you purchased it from? Potential readers can then see and use your unbiased opinion to make purchase decisions, we at Packt can understand what you think about our products, and our authors can see your feedback on their book. Thank you!

For more information about Packt, please visit `packtpub.com`.

1
Getting Started and Working with Shell Scripting

If you work with Linux, you will come across the shell. It's usually the first program you work with. **Graphical user interface** (**GUI**) usage has become very popular due to its ease of use. Those who want to take advantage of the power of Linux will use the shell program by default:

- The shell is a program that provides the user with direct interaction with the operating system. Let's understand the stages in the evolution of the Linux operating system. Linux was developed as a free and open source substitute for the Unix OS. The chronology was as follows: The Unix operating system was developed by Ken Thomson and Dennis Ritchie in 1969. It was released in 1970. They rewrote Unix using C language in 1972.
- In 1991, Linus Torvalds developed the Linux kernel for the free operating system.

In this chapter, we will cover the following topics:

- Comparison of shells
- Working in shell
- Learning basic Linux commands
- Our first script—`Hello World`
- Compiler and interpreter–differences in processes
- When not to use scripts
- Various directories
- Working more effectively with shell–basic commands
- Working with permissions

Comparison of shells

Initially, the Unix OS used a shell program called the **Bourne shell**. Then, eventually, many more shell programs were developed for different flavors of Unix. The following is some brief information about different shells:

- sh—Bourne shell
- csh—C shell
- ksh—Korn shell
- tcsh—enhanced C shell
- bash—GNU Bourne Again shell
- zsh—extension to bash, ksh, and tcsh
- pdksh—extension to ksh

A brief comparison of various shells is presented in the following table:

Feature	Bourne	C	TC	Korn	Bash
Aliases	no	yes	yes	yes	yes
Command-line editing	no	no	yes	yes	yes
Advanced pattern matching	no	no	no	yes	yes
Filename completion	no	yes	yes	yes	yes
Directory stacks (pushd and popd)	no	yes	yes	no	yes
History	no	yes	yes	yes	yes
Functions	yes	no	no	Yes	yes
Key binding	no	no	yes	no	yes
Job control	no	yes	yes	yes	yes
Spelling correction	no	no	yes	no	yes
Prompt formatting	no	no	yes	no	yes

What we see here is that, generally, the syntax of all these shells is 95% similar. In this book, we are going to follow Bash shell programming.

Tasks done by the shell

Whenever we type any text in the shell Terminal, it is the responsibility of the shell (`/bin/bash`) to execute the command properly. The activities done by the shell are as follows:

- Reading text and parsing the entered command
- Evaluating meta-characters, such as wildcards, special characters, or history characters
- Process io-redirection, pipes, and background processing
- Signal handling
- Initializing programs for execution

We will discuss the preceding topics in the subsequent chapters.

Working in the shell

Let's get started by opening the Terminal, and we will familiarize ourselves with the bash shell environment:

1. Open the Linux Terminal and type in:

```
$ echo $SHELL
/bin/bash
```

2. The preceding output in the Terminal says that the current shell is `/bin/bash`, such as the Bash shell:

```
$ bash -version
GNU bash, version 4.3.48(1)-release (x86_64-pc-linux-gnu)
Copyright (C) 2013 Free Software Foundation, Inc.
License GPLv3+: GNU GPL version 3 or later
http://gnu.org/licenses/gpl.html


This is free software; you are free to change and redistribute it.
There is NO WARRANTY, to the extent permitted by law.
```

Hereafter, we will use the word `Shell` to signify the Bash shell only. If we intend to use any other shell, then it will be specifically mentioned by name, such as `KORN` and other similar shells.

In Linux, filenames in lowercase and uppercase are different; for example, the files `Hello` and `hello` are two distinct files. This is unlike Windows, where case does not matter.

As far as possible, avoid using spaces in filenames or directory names such as:

- Wrong filename—`Hello World.txt`
- Correct filename—`Hello_World.txt` or `HelloWorld.txt`

This will make certain utilities or commands fail or not work as expected, for example, the `make` utility.

While typing in filenames or directory names of the existing files or folders, use the tab completion feature of Linux. This will make working with Linux faster.

Learning basic Linux commands

The following table lists a few basic Linux commands:

Command	Description
`$ ls`	This command is used to check the content of the directory.
`$ pwd`	This command is used to check the present working directory.
`$ mkdir work`	We will work in a separate directory called `work` in our `home` directory. Use this command to create a new directory called `work` in the current folder.
`$ cd work`	This command will change our working directory to the newly created `work` directory.
`$ pwd`	This command can be used to verify whether we moved to the expected directory.
`$ touch hello.sh`	This command is used to create a new empty file called `hello.sh` in the current folder.
`$ cp hello.sh bye.sh`	This command is used to copy one file into another file. This will copy `hello.sh` as `bye.sh`.

`$ mv bye.sh welcome.sh`	This command is used to rename a file. This will rename `bye.sh` as `welcome.sh`.
`$ ll`	This command will display detailed information about files.
`$ mv welcome.sh .welcome.sh`	Let's see some magic. Rename the file using the `mv` command and run the `ls` command.
`$ ls`	Now, the `ls` command will not display our file `.welcome.sh`. The file is hidden. Any file or directory name starting with `.` (dot) becomes hidden.
`$ ls -a`	This command is used to display hidden files.
`$ rm .welcolme.sh`	This command is used to delete the file.

If we delete any file from the GUI, such as the GUI, then it will be moved to the `/home/user/.local/share/Trash/files/` all deleted files folder.

Our first script – Hello World

Since we have learned basic commands in the Linux OS, we will now write our first shell script called `hello.sh`. You can use any editor of your choice, such as vi, gedit, nano, emacs, geany, and other similar editors. I prefer to use the vi editor:

1. Create a new `hello.sh` file as follows:

```
#!/bin/bash
# This is comment line
echo "Hello World"
ls
date
```

2. Save the newly created file.

The `#!/bin/bash` line is called the shebang line. The combination of the characters `#` and `!` is called the magic sequence. The shell uses this to call the intended shell, such as `/bin/bash` in this case. This should always be the first line in a shell script.

The next few lines in the shell script are self-explanatory:

- Any line starting with # will be treated as a comment line. An exception to this would be the first line with #!/bin/bash
- The echo command will print Hello World on the screen
- The ls command will display directory content in the console
- The date command will show the current date and time

We can execute the newly created file with the following commands:

- Technique one:

```
$ bash hello.sh
```

- Technique two:

```
$ chmod +x hello.sh
```

By running any of the preceding commands, we are adding executable permissions to our newly created file. You will learn more about file permissions later in this chapter:

```
$ ./hello.sh
```

By running the preceding command, we are executing hello.sh as the executable file. With technique one, we passed a filename as an argument to the bash shell.

The output of executing hello.sh will be as follows:

```
Hello World
hello.sh
Sun Jan 18 22:53:06 IST 2015
```

Since we have successfully executed our first script, we will proceed to develop a more advanced script, hello1.sh. Please create the new hello.sh script as follows:

```
#!/bin/bash
# This is the first Bash shell
# Scriptname : Hello1.sh
# Written by:  Ganesh Naik
echo "Hello $LOGNAME, Have a nice day !"
echo "You are working in directory `pwd`."
echo "You are working on a machine called `uname -o`."
echo "List of files in your directory is :"
ls      # List files in the present working directory
echo  "Bye for now $LOGNAME. The time is `date +%T`!"
```

The output of executing `hello.sh` will be as follows:

```
Hello student, Have a nice day !.
Your are working in directory /home/student/work.
You are working on a machine called GNU/Linux.
List of files in your directory is :
hello1.sh  hello.sh
Bye for now student. The time is 22:59:03!
```

You will learn about the `LOGNAME`, `uname`, and other similar commands as we go through the book.

Compiler and interpreter – differences in process

In any program development, the following are the two options:

- **Compilation**: Using a compiler-based language, such as C, C++, Java, and other similar languages
- **Interpreter**: Using interpreter-based languages, such as Bash shell scripting.

When we use a compiler-based language, we compile the complete source code and, as a result of compilation, we get a binary executable file. We then execute the binary to check the performance of our program.

On the other hand, when we develop the shell script, such as an interpreter-based program, every line of the program is input to the Bash shell. The lines of shell script are executed one by one sequentially. Even if the second line of a script has an error, the first line will be executed by the shell interpreter.

When not to use scripts

Shell scripts have certain advantages over compiler-based programs, such as C or C++ language. However, shell scripting has certain limitations as well.

The following are the advantages:

- Scripts are easy to write
- Scripts are quick to start and easy for debugging
- They save time in development

- Tasks of administration are automated
- No additional setup or tools are required for developing or testing shell scripts

The following are the limitations of shell scripts:

- Every line in shell script creates a new process in the operating system. When we execute the compiled program, such as a C program, it runs as a single process for the complete program.
- Since every command creates a new process, shell scripts are slow compared to compiled programs.
- Shell scripts are not suitable if heavy math operations are involved.
- There are problems with cross-platform portability.

We cannot use shell scripts in the following situations:

- Where extensive file operations are required
- Where we need data structures, such as linked lists or trees
- Where we need to generate or manipulate graphics or GUIs
- Where we need direct access to system hardware
- Where we need a port or socket I/O
- Where we need to use libraries or interface with legacy code
- Where proprietary, closed source applications are used (shell scripts put the source code right out in the open for the entire world to see)

Various directories

We will explore the directory structure in Linux so that it will be useful later on:

- `/bin/`: This contains commands used by a regular user.
- `/boot/`: The files required for the operating system startup are stored here.
- `/cdrom/`: When a CD-ROM is mounted, the CD-ROM files are accessible here.
- `/dev/`: The device driver files are stored in this folder. These device driver files will point to hardware-related programs running in the kernel.
- `/etc/`: This folder contains configuration files and startup scripts.

- `/home/`: This folder contains a home folder of all users, except the administrator.
- `/lib/`: The library files are stored in this folder.
- `/media/`: External media, such as a USB pen drive, are mounted in this folder.
- `/opt/`: The optional packages are installed in this folder.
- `/proc/`: This contains files that give information about the kernel and every process running in the OS.
- `/root/`: This is the administrator's home folder.
- `/sbin/`: This contains commands used by the administrator or root user.
- `/usr/`: This contains secondary programs, libraries, and documentation about user-related programs.
- `/var/`: This contains variable data, such as HTTP, TFTP, logs, and others.
- `/sys/`: This dynamically creates the `sys` files.

Working more effectively with Shell – basic commands

Let's learn a few commands that are required very often, such as `man`, `echo`, `cat`, and similar:

- Enter the following command. It will show the various types of manual pages displayed by the `man` command:

```
$ man man
```

- From the following table, you can get an idea about various types of `man` pages for the same command:

Section number	Subject area
1	User commands
2	System calls
3	Library calls
4	Special files
5	File formats
6	Games
7	Miscellaneous

8   System admin

9   Kernel routines

- We can enter the man command to display the corresponding manual pages as follows:

```
$ man 1 command
$ man 5 command
```

- Suppose we need to know more about the passwd command, which is used for changing the current password of a user. You can type the command as follows:

```
$ man command
  man -k passwd    // show all pages with keyword
  man -K passwd    // will search all manual pages content for pattern
"passwd"
$ man passwd
```

- This will show information about the passwd command:

```
$ man 5 passwd
```

- The preceding command will give information about the file passwd, which is stored in the /etc/ folder, such as /etc/passwd.

- We can get brief information about the command as follows:

```
$ whatis passwd
```

- Output:

```
passwd (1ssl)       - compute password hashes
passwd (1)          - change user password
passwd (5)          - the password file
```

- Every command we type in the Terminal has an executable binary program file associated with it. We can check the location of a binary file as follows:

```
$ which passwd
/usr/bin/passwd
```

- The preceding line tells us that the binary file of the passwd command is located in the /usr/bin/passwd folder.

- We can get complete information about the binary file location, as well as the manual page location of any command, with the following:

```
$ whereis passwd
```

- The output will be as follows:

```
passwd: /usr/bin/passwd /etc/passwd /usr/bin/X11/passwd
/usr/share/man/man1/passwd.1.gz /usr/share/man/man1/passwd.1ssl.gz
/usr/share/man/man5/passwd.5.gz
```

- Change the user login and effective username:

```
$ whoami
```

- This command displays the username of the logged in user:

```
$ su
```

- The su (switch user) command will make the user the administrator but you should know the administrator's password. The sudo (superuser do) command will run the command with administrator privileges. The user should have been added to the sudoers list.

```
# who am i
```

- This command will show the effective user who is working at that moment.

```
# exit
```

- Many a times, you might need to create new commands from existing commands. Sometimes, existing commands have complex options to remember. In such cases, we can create new commands as follows:

```
$ alias ll='ls -l'
$ alias copy='cp -rf'
```

- To list all declared aliases, use the following command:

```
$ alias
```

- To remove an alias, use the following command:

```
$ unalias copy
```

- We can check operating system details, such as UNIX/Linux or the distribution that is installed with the following command:

```
$ uname
```

- Output:

```
Linux
```

  This will display the basic OS information (Unix name)

- Linux kernel version information will be displayed by the following:

```
$ uname -r
```

- Output:

```
3.13.0-32-generic
```

- To get all the information about a Linux machine, use the following command:

```
$ uname -a
```

- Output:

```
Linux localhost.localdomain 3.10.0-693.el7.x86_64 #1 SMP Tue Aug 22
21:09:27 UTC 2017 x86_64 x86_64 x86_64 GNU/Linux
```

- The following commands will give you more information about the Linux distribution:

```
$ cat /proc/version    // detailed info about distribution
$ cat /etc/*release
# lsb_release -a
.
```

```
[student@localhost ~]$ lsb_release -a
LSB Version:     :core-4.1-amd64:core-4.1-noarch:cxx-4.1-amd64:cxx-4.1-noarch:desktop
-4.1-amd64:desktop-4.1-noarch:languages-4.1-amd64:languages-4.1-noarch:printing-4.1-
amd64:printing-4.1-noarch
Distributor ID: CentOS
Description:    CentOS Linux release 7.4.1708 (Core)
Release:        7.4.1708
Codename:       Core
```

- The `cat` command is used for reading files and is displayed on the standard output.

- Sometimes, we need to copy a file or directory to many places. In such situations, instead of copying the original file or directory again and again, we can create soft links. In Windows, it is a similar feature to creating a shortcut.

```
$ ln -s file file_link
```

- To learn about the type of file, you can use the command file. In Linux, various types of file exist. Some examples are as follows:
    - Regular file (-)
    - Directory (d)
    - Soft link (l)
    - Character device driver (c)
    - Block device driver (b)
    - Pipe file (p)
    - Socket file (s)
- We can get information about a file using the following command:

```
$ file file_name
```

- Printing some text on screen for showing results to the user, or to ask for details is an essential activity.
- The following command will create a new file called file_name using the cat command:

```
$ cat > file_name
line 1
line 2
line 3
< Cntrl + D will save the file    >
```

- But this is very rarely used, as many powerful editors already exist, such as vi or gedit.
- The following command will print Hello World on the console. The echo command is very useful for shell script writers:

```
$ echo "Hello World"
```

```
$ echo "Hello World" > hello.sh
```

- The `echo` command with > overwrites the content of the file. If the content already exists in the file, it will be deleted and new content added. In situations where we need to append the text to the file, then we can use the `echo` command as follows:

`$ echo "Hello World" >> hello.sh  will append the text`

- The following command will copy the `Hello World` string to the `hello.sh` file:
- The following command will display the content of the file on screen:

`$ cat hello.sh`

Working with permissions

The following are the types of permissions:

- **Read permission**: The user can read or check the content of the file
- **Write permission**: The user can edit or modify the file
- **Execute permission**: The user can execute the file

Changing file permissions

The following are the commands for changing file permissions:

To check the file permission, enter the following command:

`$ ll file_name`

The file permission details are as seen in the following diagram:

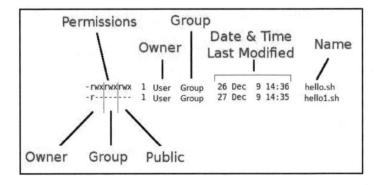

In the preceding diagram, as we can see, permissions are grouped in owner-user, group, and other users' permissions. Permissions are of three types–read, write, and execute. As per the requirement, we may need to change the permissions of the various files.

The chmod command

We can change the file or directory permissions in the following two ways:

Technique one – the symbolic method

The following command will add the read/write and execute permissions to the file wherein u is for user, g is for group, and o is for others:

```
$ chmod ugo+rwx file_name
```

Alternatively, you can use the following command:

```
$ chmod +rwx file_name
```

Technique two – the numeric method

The following command will change the file permissions using the octal technique:

```
$ chmod 777 file_name
```

The file permission 777 can be understood as 111 111 111, which corresponds to the rwx.rwx.rwx permissions.

Setting umask

We will see how Linux decides the default permissions of the newly created file or folder:

```
$ umask
0002
```

The meaning of the preceding output is that, if we create a new directory, then, from the permissions of +rwx, the permission 0002 will be subtracted. This means that for a newly created directory, the permissions will be 775, or rwx rwx r-x. For a newly created file, the file permissions will be rw- rw- r--. By default, for any newly created text file, the execute bit will never be set. Therefore, the newly created text file and the directory will have different permissions, even though umask is the same.

Setuid

Another very interesting functionality is the setuid feature. If the setuid bit is set for a script, then the script will always run with the owner's privileges, irrespective of which user is running the script. If the administrator wants to run a script written by him by other users, then he can set this bit.

Consider either of the following situations:

```
$ chmod u+s file_name
$ chmod 4777 file
```

The file permissions after any of the preceding two commands will be drwsrwxrwx.

Setgid

Similar to setuid, the setgid functionality gives the user the ability to run scripts with a group owner's privileges, even if it is executed by any other user:

```
$ chmod g+s filename
```

Alternatively, you can use the following command:

```
$ chmod 2777 filename
```

File permissions after any of the preceding two commands will be drwxrwsrwtx.

Sticky bit

The sticky bit is a very interesting functionality. Let's say, in the administration department, there are 10 users. If one folder has been set with sticky bit, then all other users can copy files to that folder. All users can read the files, but only the owner of the respective file can edit or delete the file. Other users can only read, but not edit or modify, the files if the sticky bit is set:

```
$ chmod +t filename
```

Alternatively, you can use the following command:

```
$ chmod 1777
```

File permissions after any of the preceding two commands will be `drwxrwxrwt`.

Summary

In this chapter, you learned different ways to write and run shell scripts. You also learned ways to handle files and directories, as well as work with permissions.

In the next chapter, you will learn about process management, job control, and automation.

2
Drilling Deep into Process Management, Job Control, and Automation

In the last chapter, we introduced ourselves to the Bash shell environment in Linux. You learned basic commands and wrote your first shell script as well.

You also learned about process management and job control. This information will be very useful for system administrators in automation and in terms of solving many problems.

In this chapter, we will cover the following topics:

- Monitoring processes with `ps`
- Job management–working with `fg`, `bg`, `jobs`, and `kill`
- Exploring `at` and `crontab`

Introducing process basics

A running instance of a program is called a process. A program stored in the hard disk or pen drive is not a process. When that stored program starts executing, then we say that process has been created and is running.

Let's very briefly understand the Linux operating system boot-up sequence:

1. In PCs, initially, the BIOS chip initializes system hardware, such as PCI bus, and display device drivers.
2. Then the BIOS executes the boot loader program.

3. The boot loader program then copies the kernel in the memory and, after basic checks, it calls a kernel function `start_kernel()`.

4. The kernel then initializes the OS and creates the first process called `init`.

5. You can check the presence of this process with the following command:

```
$ ps -ef
```

6. Every process in the OS has one numerical identification associated with it. It is called a `process ID`. The process ID of the `init` process is `1`. This process is the parent process of all user space processes.

7. In the Linux OS, every new process is created by a system call called `fork()`.

8. Therefore, every process has a process ID, as well as the parent process ID.

9. We can see the complete process tree using the following command:

```
$ pstree
```

You can see the very first process as `init`, as well as all other processes with a complete parent and child relation between them. If we use the `$ps -ef` command, then we can see that the `init` process is owned by the root and its parent process ID is `0`. This means that there is no parent for `init`:

```
[student@localhost ~]$ pstree
systemd─┬─ModemManager───2*[{ModemManager}]
        ├─NetworkManager───2*[{NetworkManager}]
        ├─VGAuthService
        ├─abrt-dbus───2*[{abrt-dbus}]
        ├─2*[abrt-watch-log]
        ├─abrtd
        ├─accounts-daemon───2*[{accounts-daemon}]
        ├─alsactl
        ├─at-spi-bus-laun─┬─dbus-daemon───{dbus-daemon}
        │                 └─3*[{at-spi-bus-laun}]
        ├─at-spi2-registr───2*[{at-spi2-registr}]
        ├─atd
        ├─auditd─┬─audispd─┬─sedispatch
        │        │         └─{audispd}
        │        └─{auditd}
        ├─avahi-daemon───avahi-daemon
        ├─chronyd
        ├─colord───2*[{colord}]
        ├─crond
        ├─cupsd
        ├─2*[dbus-daemon───{dbus-daemon}]
        ├─dbus-launch
        ├─dconf-service───2*[{dconf-service}]
```

Therefore, with the exception of the `init` process, all other processes are created by some other process. The `init` process is created by the kernel itself.

The following are the different types of processes:

- **Orphan process**: If, by some chance, the parent process is terminated, then the child process becomes an orphan process. The process that created the parent process, such as the grandparent process, becomes the parent of the orphan child process. As a last resort, the `init` process becomes the parent of the orphan process.

- **Zombie process**: Every process has one data structure called the process control table. This is maintained in the operating system. This table contains information about all the child processes created by the parent process. If, by chance, the parent process is sleeping or is suspended due to some reason or other and the child process is terminated, then the parent process cannot receive the information about the child process termination. In such cases, the child process that has been terminated is called the zombie process. When the parent process awakes, it will receive a signal regarding the child process termination and the process control block data structure will be updated. The child process termination is then completed.

- **Daemon process**: Until now, we have started every new process in a Bash Terminal. Therefore, if we print any text with the `$ echo` command, it will be printed in the Terminal itself. There are certain processes that are not associated with any Terminal. Such a process is called a daemon process. These processes are running in the background. An advantage of the daemon process is that it is immune to the changes happening to the Bash shell that has created it. When we want to run certain background processes, such as a DHCP server, then the daemon process is very useful.

Monitoring processes using ps

We have used the `ps` command in the introduction. Let's learn more about it:

- To list the processes associated with our current Bash shell Terminal, enter the following command:

`$ ps`

```
[student@localhost ~]$
[student@localhost ~]$ ps
  PID TTY          TIME CMD
 7853 pts/0    00:00:00 bash
 8546 pts/0    00:00:00 ps
[student@localhost ~]$
[student@localhost ~]$
```

- To list processes, along with the parent process ID associated with the current Terminal, enter the following command:

`$ ps -f`

```
[student@localhost ~]$
[student@localhost ~]$
[student@localhost ~]$ ps -f
UID         PID    PPID  C STIME TTY          TIME CMD
student    7853    7846  0 13:19 pts/0    00:00:00 bash
student    8673    7853  0 14:04 pts/0    00:00:00 ps -f
[student@localhost ~]$
[student@localhost ~]$
```

- We can see the process ID in the `PID` column and the parent process ID, in the `PPID` column in the preceding output.

- To list processes with the parent process ID along with the process state, enter the following command:

`$ ps -lf`

```
[student@localhost ~]$
[student@localhost ~]$
[student@localhost ~]$ ps -lf
F S UID         PID    PPID  C PRI  NI ADDR SZ WCHAN  STIME TTY          TIME CMD
0 S student    7853    7846  0  80   0 - 29174 do_wai 13:19 pts/0    00:00:00 bas
0 R student    8715    7853  0  80   0 - 37766 -      14:06 pts/0    00:00:00 ps
[student@localhost ~]$
[student@localhost ~]$
[student@localhost ~]$
```

- In the preceding output, the column with S (state) shows the current state of a process, such as R for running and S for suspended state.

- To list all the processes running in the operating system, including the system processes, enter the following command:

```
$ ps -ef
```

```
[student@localhost ~]$
[student@localhost ~]$ ps -ef
UID        PID  PPID  C STIME TTY          TIME CMD
root         1     0  0 10:16 ?        00:00:04 /usr/lib/systemd/systemd --switched-root
root         2     0  0 10:16 ?        00:00:00 [kthreadd]
root         3     2  0 10:16 ?        00:00:00 [ksoftirqd/0]
root         5     2  0 10:16 ?        00:00:00 [kworker/0:0H]
root         7     2  0 10:16 ?        00:00:00 [migration/0]
root         8     2  0 10:16 ?        00:00:00 [rcu_bh]
root         9     2  0 10:16 ?        00:00:01 [rcu_sched]
root        10     2  0 10:16 ?        00:00:00 [watchdog/0]
root        12     2  0 10:16 ?        00:00:00 [kdevtmpfs]
root        13     2  0 10:16 ?        00:00:00 [netns]
root        14     2  0 10:16 ?        00:00:00 [khungtaskd]
root        15     2  0 10:16 ?        00:00:00 [writeback]
root        16     2  0 10:16 ?        00:00:00 [kintegrityd]
root        17     2  0 10:16 ?        00:00:00 [bioset]
root        18     2  0 10:16 ?        00:00:00 [kblockd]
root        19     2  0 10:16 ?        00:00:00 [md]
root        25     2  0 10:16 ?        00:00:00 [kswapd0]
root        26     2  0 10:16 ?        00:00:00 [ksmd]
root        27     2  0 10:16 ?        00:00:00 [khugepaged]
root        28     2  0 10:16 ?        00:00:00 [crypto]
root        36     2  0 10:16 ?        00:00:00 [kthrotld]
root        38     2  0 10:16 ?        00:00:00 [kmpath_rdacd]
root        39     2  0 10:16 ?        00:00:00 [kpsmoused]
```

- The process names in [] are kernel threads. If you are interested in more options for the ps command, you can use the following command:

```
$ man ps
```

- To find a particular process, you can use the following command:

```
$ ps -ef | grep "process_name"
```

- The command with grep will display the process with process_name.

- If we want to terminate the running process, enter the following command:

```
$ kill   pid_of_process_to_be_killed
```

```
[student@localhost ~]$
[student@localhost ~]$ ps
   PID TTY          TIME CMD
  9508 pts/0    00:00:00 bash
  9555 pts/0    00:00:00 sleep
  9575 pts/0    00:00:00 ps
[student@localhost ~]$
[student@localhost ~]$ kill 9555
[1]+  Terminated              sleep 10000
[student@localhost ~]$
[student@localhost ~]$ ps
   PID TTY          TIME CMD
  9508 pts/0    00:00:00 bash
  9609 pts/0    00:00:00 ps
[student@localhost ~]$
```

- Many a time, if the process is not killed by the `$ kill` command, you may need to pass additional options to ensure that the required process is killed, which is shown as follows:

```
$ kill -9 pid_of_process_to_be_killed
```

- We can terminate the process with the name of a process, instead of using the process ID, as follows:

```
$ pkill command_name
$ pkill sleep
```

- Or:

```
$ pkill   -9   command_name
```

```
[student@localhost ~]$
[student@localhost ~]$ ps
   PID TTY          TIME CMD
  3089 pts/0    00:00:00 bash
  3305 pts/0    00:00:00 sleep
  3318 pts/0    00:00:00 ps
[student@localhost ~]$
[student@localhost ~]$ pkill sleep
pkill: killing pid 3298 failed: Operation not permitted
[1]+  Terminated              sleep 10000
[student@localhost ~]$
[student@localhost ~]$ ps
   PID TTY          TIME CMD
  3089 pts/0    00:00:00 bash
  3344 pts/0    00:00:00 ps
[student@localhost ~]$
[student@localhost ~]$
```

- To know more about various flags of `kill`, enter the following command:

`$ kill -l`

- This displays all the signals or software interrupts used by the operating system. When we enter the `$ kill` command, the operating system sends the `SIGTERM` signal to the process.
- If the process is not killed by this command, then we enter the following command:

`$ kill -9 process_name`

- This sends `SIGKILL` to the process to be killed.

Process management

Since we have understood the command to check processes, we will learn more about managing different processes.

- In a Bash shell, when we enter any command or start any program, it starts running in the foreground. In such a situation, we cannot run more than one command in the foreground. We need to create many Terminal windows for starting many processes. If we need to start many processes or programs from the same Terminal, then we will need to start them as background processes.
- If we want to start a process in the background, then we need to append the command in the Bash shell by `&`.
- If I want to start my `Hello` program as the background process, then the command would be as follows:

`$ Hello &`

- If we terminate any command by `&`, then it starts running as the background process.

For example, we will issue a simple `sleep` command, which creates a new process. This process sleeps for the duration, which is mentioned in the integer value next to the `sleep` command:

1. The following command will make the process sleep for 10,000 seconds. This means we will not be able to run any other command from the same Terminal:

```
$ sleep 10000
```

2. Now, you can press the *Ctrl + C* key combination to terminate the process created by the `sleep` command.

```
[student@localhost ~]$
[student@localhost ~]$ ps
  PID TTY          TIME CMD
 3089 pts/0    00:00:00 bash
 3729 pts/0    00:00:00 ps
[student@localhost ~]$
[student@localhost ~]$
[student@localhost ~]$ sleep 10000

^C
[student@localhost ~]$
[student@localhost ~]$
```

3. Now, use the following command:

```
$ sleep 10000 &
```

The preceding command will create a new process, which will be put to sleep for `10000` seconds; but this time, it will start running in the background. Therefore, we will be able to enter the next command in the Bash Terminal.

4. Since the newly created process is running in the background, we can enter new commands very easily in the same Terminal window:

```
$ sleep 20000 &
$ sleep 30000 &
$ sleep 40000 &
```

5. To check the presence of all the processes, enter the following command:

```
$ jobs
```

```
[student@localhost ~]$
[student@localhost ~]$ sleep 10000 &
[1] 4419
[student@localhost ~]$ sleep 20000 &
[2] 4426
[student@localhost ~]$ sleep 30000 &
[3] 4433
[student@localhost ~]$ sleep 40000 &
[4] 4440
[student@localhost ~]$ jobs
[1]   Running                 sleep 10000 &
[2]   Running                 sleep 20000 &
[3]-  Running                 sleep 30000 &
[4]+  Running                 sleep 40000 &
[student@localhost ~]$
[student@localhost ~]$
```

The `jobs` command lists all the processes running in the Terminal, including foreground and background processes. You can clearly see their status as running, suspended, or stopped. The numbers in `[]` show the job ID. The + sign indicates which command will receive `fg` and `bg` commands by default. We will study them in the following topics.

6. If you want to make any existing background process run in the foreground, then use the following command:

   `$ fg 3`

   The preceding command will make the job number 3 run in the foreground instead of the background.

   If we want to make the process stop executing and get it suspended, then press *Ctrl* + Z. This key combination makes the foreground process stop executing. Please note that the process has stopped, but is not terminated.

```
[student@localhost ~]$ fg 3
sleep 30000

^Z
[3]+  Stopped                 sleep 30000
[student@localhost ~]$
[student@localhost ~]$ jobs
[1]   Running                 sleep 10000 &
[2]   Running                 sleep 20000 &
[3]+  Stopped                 sleep 30000
[4]-  Running                 sleep 40000 &
[student@localhost ~]$
```

7. To make the stopped process continue running in the background, use the following command:

```
$ bg job_number
$ bg 3
```

The preceding command will make suspended job process number 3 run in the background.

8. If you wish to terminate the process, you can use the job ID or process ID as follows:

```
$ jobs -l        //  This will list jobs with pid
$ kill pid        // or
$ kill %job_id    // This will kill job
$ kill %3
```

Process monitoring tools – top, iostat, and vmstat

We can view the native performance of various processes in an OS by using the following tools:

- To view a dynamic real-time view of the running processes in an OS, use the following command:

```
$ top
```

```
top - 16:40:34 up  1:07,  2 users,  load average: 0.25, 0.12, 0.08
Tasks: 180 total,   1 running, 178 sleeping,   1 stopped,   0 zombie
%Cpu(s):  1.4 us,  0.3 sy,  0.0 ni, 98.3 id,  0.0 wa,  0.0 hi,  0.0 si,  0.0 st
KiB Mem :  1867024 total,   615620 free,   726984 used,   524420 buff/cache
KiB Swap:  2097148 total,  2097148 free,        0 used.   925896 avail Mem

  PID USER      PR  NI    VIRT    RES    SHR S %CPU %MEM     TIME+ COMMAND
 2426 student   20   0 1890548 191072  48088 S  2.0 10.2   0:18.09 gnome-shell
 1764 root      20   0  289548  32460  10200 S  1.0  1.7   0:04.18 X
 4345 student   20   0  708344  22420  14360 S  0.7  1.2   0:00.56 gnome-terminal-
  401 root      20   0       0      0      0 S  0.3  0.0   0:00.72 xfsaild/dm-0
 1099 root      20   0  231348   6104   4752 S  0.3  0.3   0:04.14 vmtoolsd
 1489 root      20   0  562344  16588   5880 S  0.3  0.9   0:00.65 tuned
 4587 student   20   0  157716   2236   1532 R  0.3  0.1   0:00.07 top
    1 root      20   0  128436   7232   4064 S  0.0  0.4   0:01.90 systemd
    2 root      20   0       0      0      0 S  0.0  0.0   0:00.00 kthreadd
    3 root      20   0       0      0      0 S  0.0  0.0   0:00.11 ksoftirqd/0
    5 root       0 -20       0      0      0 S  0.0  0.0   0:00.00 kworker/0:0H
    7 root      rt   0       0      0      0 S  0.0  0.0   0:00.00 migration/0
    8 root      20   0       0      0      0 S  0.0  0.0   0:00.00 rcu_bh
    9 root      20   0       0      0      0 S  0.0  0.0   0:00.41 rcu_sched
   10 root      rt   0       0      0      0 S  0.0  0.0   0:00.02 watchdog/0
   12 root      20   0       0      0      0 S  0.0  0.0   0:00.00 kdevtmpfs
   13 root       0 -20       0      0      0 S  0.0  0.0   0:00.00 netns
   14 root      20   0       0      0      0 S  0.0  0.0   0:00.00 khungtaskd
   15 root       0 -20       0      0      0 S  0.0  0.0   0:00.00 writeback
   16 root       0 -20       0      0      0 S  0.0  0.0   0:00.00 kintegrityd
   17 root       0 -20       0      0      0 S  0.0  0.0   0:00.00 bioset
   18 root       0 -20       0      0      0 S  0.0  0.0   0:00.00 kblockd
```

An explanation of the `top` command generated output is as follows:

The `$top` command displays a lot of information about the running system.

The first line of the display is shown as follows:

```
top - 16:53:10 up  1:19,  2 users,  load average: 0.17, 0.13, 0.09
```

The description of fields in the first line is as follows:

- Current time
- System uptime
- Number of users logged in
- Load average of 5, 10, and 15 minutes, respectively

The second line is shown as follows:

```
Tasks: 181 total,   1 running, 179 sleeping,   1 stopped,   0 zombie
```

This line shows the summary of tasks or processes. It shows the total number of all the processes, which includes the total number of running, sleeping, stopped, and zombie processes. The third line is shown as follows:

```
%Cpu(s):  0.3 us,  0.0 sy,  0.0 ni, 99.7 id,  0.0 wa,  0.0 hi,  0.0 si,  0.0 st
```

This line shows information about CPU usage as a % in different modes as follows:

- * us (user): CPU usage in % for running (un-niced) user processes
- * sy (system): CPU usage in % for running kernel processes
- * ni (niced): CPU usage in % for running niced user processes
- * wa (IO wait): CPU usage in % waiting for IO completion
- * hi (hardware interrupts): CPU usage in % for serving hardware interrupts
- * si (software interrupts): CPU usage in % for serving software interrupts
- * st (time stolen): CPU usage in % for time stolen for this VM by the hypervisor

The fourth line is shown as follows:

```
KiB Mem :  1867024 total,   612492 free,   729876 used,   524656 buff/cache
KiB Swap:  2097148 total,  2097148 free,        0 used.   922884 avail Mem
```

This line provides information about memory usage. It shows the physical memory that is used, free, available, and used for buffers. The next line shows the swap memory that is available, used, free, and cached.

After this line, we see the table of values with the following columns:

- PID: This is the ID of the process
- USER: This is the user that is the owner of the process
- PR: This is the priority of the process
- NI: This is the NICE value of the process
- VIRT: This is the virtual memory used by the process
- RES: This is the physical memory used for the process

- SHR: This is the shared memory of the process
- S: This indicates the status of the process: S = sleep, R = running, and Z = zombie (S)
- %CPU: This is the % of CPU used by this process
- %MEM: This is the % of RAM used by the process
- TIME+: This is the total time of activity of this process
- COMMAND: This is the name of the process

Let's take a look at the performance monitoring tools iostat, vmstat, and sar:

- To view the statistics of the CPU and the input/output device's utilization, use the following command:

  $ **iostat**

```
[student@localhost ~]$ iostat
Linux 3.10.0-693.el7.x86_64 (localhost.localdomain)      Thursday 28 December 2017      _x86_64_      (1 CPU)

avg-cpu:  %user   %nice %system %iowait  %steal   %idle
           0.74    0.48    1.27    1.34    0.00   96.16

Device:            tps    kB_read/s    kB_wrtn/s    kB_read    kB_wrtn
sda               9.55       554.05         9.86    1333552      23732
scd0              0.01         0.44         0.00       1050          0
dm-0              9.11       539.71         9.00    1299043      21664
dm-1              0.04         0.93         0.00       2228          0

[student@localhost ~]$
```

  $ **iostat -c**

- Shows only CPU statistics

  $ **iostat -d**

- Shows only disk statistics

- To view the virtual memory statistics, use the following command:

  $**vmstat**

```
[student@localhost ~]$ vmstat
procs -----------memory---------- ---swap-- -----io---- -system-- ------cpu-----
 r  b   swpd   free   buff  cache   si   so    bi    bo   in   cs us sy id wa st
 3  0     12  82260    208 955868    0    0   440    13  122  203  1  1 97  1  0
[student@localhost ~]$
```

  $ **vmstat -s**

- This shows various event counters and memory statistics

```
$ vmstat -t 1 5
```

- Runs for every one second stop after executing for five intervals

```
$ sar -u 2 3
```

- This will show the CPU activity report three times every 2 seconds:

```
[student@localhost ~]$ sar -u 2 3
Linux 3.10.0-693.el7.x86_64 (localhost.localdomain)      Thursday 28 December 2017  _x86_64_  (1 CPU)

12:16:07  IST     CPU     %user    %nice   %system   %iowait   %steal    %idle
12:16:09  IST     all      1.04     0.00      1.55      0.00     0.00     97.41
12:16:11  IST     all      1.03     0.00      0.00      0.00     0.00     98.97
12:16:13  IST     all      1.03     0.00      0.52      0.00     0.00     98.45
Average:          all      1.03     0.00      0.69      0.00     0.00     98.28
[student@localhost ~]$
```

Understanding "at"

Many a time, we need to schedule a task for a future time, say in the evening at 8 p.m. on a specific day. We can use the at command in such a situation.

Sometimes, we need to repeat the same task at a specific time, periodically, every day, or every month. In such situations, we can use the crontab command.

Let's learn more about the use of the at command. To use the at command, the syntax is as follows:

```
$ at time date
```

The following are examples of the at command:

- The *Ctrl + D* command will save the at job. The task will be executed at 11.15 A.M. This command will log messages to the log.txt file at 11.15 a.m.:

```
$ at 11.15 AM
at >   echo "Hello World" > $HOME/log.txt
at >   Control + D
```

- The following command will send an email on March 31, 2015, at 10 A.M.:

```
$ at 10am mar 31 2015
at> echo "taxes due" | mail jon
at> ^D
```

- The following command will make the task run on May 20 at 11 A.M.:

```
$ at 11 am may 20
```

- All the jobs that are scheduled by the `at` command can be listed using the following command:

```
$ atq
```

- To remove a specific job listed by the `atq` command, we can use the following command:

```
$ atrm  job-id
```

Understanding crontab

If we need to run a specific task repetitively, then the solution is to use `crontab`. The syntax of the command is as follows:

```
$ crontab -e
```

This will open a new editor. The following diagram is the syntax to add tasks. The fields to use for repeating tasks at a particular time are explained here:

Finally, to save the jobs, use the following:

```
Press Esc then type :wq
```

The preceding operations will save the job and quit crontab.

The following are a few examples of the `crontab` command:

- Use the following command to run a script every hour at the fifth minute, every day:

```
5 * * * *        $HOME/bin/daily.job >> $HOME/tmp/out  2>&1
```

- Use the following command to run 5 minutes after midnight every day:

```
5 0 * * *        $HOME/bin/daily.job >> $HOME/tmp/out  2>&1
```

- Use the following command to run at 2.15 p.m. on the first of every month–the output is mailed to Paul:

```
15 14 1 * * *     $HOME/bin/monthly
```

- Use the following command to run at 10 P.M. on weekdays, and send the email to ganesh@abc.com:

```
0 22 * *  1-5   sendmail ganesh@abc.com  < ~/work/email.txt
```

- The `sendmail` utility is used for sending emails. We can also use the mail utility as follows:

```
sendmail user@example.com  < /tmp/email.txt
```

- The following commands are self-explanatory from the text of the `echo` command:

```
23 0-23/2  *  *  *  echo "run 23 minutes after midn, 2 am, 4 am,
everyday"
    5  4  *  *  sun   echo "run at 5 minutes after 4 am every Sunday"
```

The following are a few more `crontab` command examples:

Min	Hour	Day / month	Month	Day / week	Execution time
45	0	5	1,6,12	*	00:45 hrs on the fifth day of January, June, and December.
0	18	*	10	1-5	6.00 P.M. every weekday (Monday-Friday), only in October.
0	0	1,10,15	*	*	Midnight on the first, tenth, and fifteenth days of the month.
5,10	0	10	*	1	At 12.05 and 12.10 every Monday, and on the tenth day of every month.

We can add `macros` in the `crontab` file. Use the following to restart `my_program` after each reboot:

```
@reboot  /bin/my_program
@reboot echo `hostname` was rebooted at `date` | mail -s "Reboot
notification" ganesh.admin@some-corp.com
```

The following is a summary of a few more macros:

Entry	Description	Equivalent To
@reboot	Run once at start-up	None
@weekly	Run once a week	0 0 * * 0
@daily	Run once a day	0 0 * * *
@midnight	(same as @daily)	0 0 * * *
@hourly	Run once an hour	0 * * * *

Summary

In this chapter, we studied basic process management. You learned about the ps command. Using commands such as jobs, fg, bg, kill, and pkill, we studied job management. Later on, you learned about the top, iostat, and vmstat process monitoring tools.

In the next chapter, you will learn about standard input/output, various meta–characters, and text filters used in shell scripting.

3
Using Text Processing and Filters in Your Scripts

In the last chapter, you studied basic process management. You learned about the `ps` command. You also studied job management by using commands such as `jobs`, `fg`, `bg`, `kill`, and `pkill`, as well as various other tools, such as `top`, `iostat`, and `vmstat`. In this chapter, we will cover the following topics:

- Using `more`, `less`, `head`, and `tail`
- Using `diff`, `cut`, `paste`, `comm`, and `uniq`
- Working with `grep`
- Understanding standard input, standard output, and standard error
- Understanding various meta-characters and their usage

Text filtering tools

Normally, shell scripting involves report generation, which will include processing various text files and filtering their output to finally produce the desired results. Let's start discussing the two Linux commands, namely `more` and `less`:

- `more`: Sometimes we get a very large output on the screen for certain commands, which cannot be viewed completely in one screen. In such cases, we can use the `more` command to view the output text one page at a time. Add | `more` after the command, as follows:

```
$ ll /dev | more
```

   The | is called a pipe. You will learn more about it in the next chapters. In this command, pressing the spacebar will move the output on the screen one page at a time, or pressing Enter will move the screen one line at a time.

- `less`: Instead of more, if you use `less`, it will show a screen containing the full text all at once. We can move forward as well as backward. This is a very useful text-filtering tool.

  The syntax usage is as follows:

```
$ command |  less
e.g. $ ll /proc | less
```

This command will show a long directory listing of the `/proc` folder. Let's say that we want to see whether the `cpuinfo` file is present in the directory. Just press the arrow key up or down to scroll through the display. With the `more` command, you cannot scroll backward. You can move forward only. With page up and down key presses, you can move forward or backward one page at a time, which is very fast. In addition to scrolling forward or backward, you can search for a pattern using `/` for forward search and `?` for backward search. You can use `N` for repeating the search in a forward or backward direction.

Head and tail

For testing the next few commands, we will need a file with a sequence of numbers from 1 to 100. For this, use the following command:

```
$ seq 100 > numbers.txt
```

The preceding command creates a file with the numbers 1 to 100 on separate lines. The following example shows the usage of the `head` command:

```
$ head numbers.txt      // will display 10 lines
$ head -3 numbers.txt   // will show first 3 lines
$ head +5 numbers.txt   // will show from line 5. In few shells this
command may not work
```

The following example shows the usage of the `tail` command:

```
$ tail numbers.txt       // will display last 10 lines
$ tail -5  numbers.txt      // will show last 5 lines
$ tail +15 numbers.txt  // will show from line 15 onwards. In few
shells this may not work
```

To print lines 61 to 65 from `numbers.txt` into file `log.txt`, type the following:

```
$ head -65 numbers.txt | tail -5 > log.txt
```

The diff command

The `diff` command is used to find differences between two files. Let's see a few examples to find out its usage. The content of `file1` is as follows:

```
I go for shopping on Saturday
I rest completely on Sunday
I use Facebook & Twitter for social networking
```

The content of `file2` is as follows:

```
Today is Monday.
I go for shopping on Saturday
I rest completely on Sunday
I use Facebook & Twitter for social networking
```

Type the `diff` command:

```
$ diff file1 file2
```

The output will be this:

```
0a1
> Today is Monday
```

In the output, `0a1` tells us that line number 1 is added in `file2`. Let's see another example with line deletion. The content of `file1` is as follows:

```
Today is Monday
I go for shopping on Saturday
I rest completely on Sunday
I use Facebook & Twitter for social networking
```

The content of `file2` is as follows:

```
Today is Monday
I go for shopping on Saturday
I rest completely on Sunday
```

Type the `diff` command:

```
$ diff file1 file2
```

The output is as follows:

```
4d3
< I use Facebook & Tweeter for social networking.
```

In the output, 4d3 tells us that line number 4 is deleted in file2. Similarly, the c command will show us changes to a file as well.

The cut command

The cut command is used to extract specified columns/characters of a piece of text, which is given as follows:

- -c: Specifies the filtering of characters
- -d: Specifies the delimiter for fields
- -f: Specifies the field number

The following are a few examples that show the usage of the cut command:

- Using the next command, from the /etc/passwd file, fields 1 and 3 will be displayed. The display will contain the login name and user ID. We use the -d: option to specify that the field or columns are separated by a colon (:):

```
$ cut -d: -f1,3 /etc/passwd
```

```
[student@localhost ~]$ cut -d: -f1,3 /etc/passwd
root:0
bin:1
daemon:2
adm:3
lp:4
sync:5
shutdown:6
halt:7
mail:8
operator:11
games:12
ftp:14
nobody:99
ods:999
pegasus:66
systemd-network:192
dbus:81
polkitd:998
apache:48
tomcat:91
colord:997
abrt:173
saslauth:996
```

- Using this command, from the /etc/passwd file, the fields 1 to 5 will be displayed. The display will contain the login name, encrypted password, user ID, group ID, and user name:

```
$ cut -d: -f1-5 /etc/passwd
```

```
[student@localhost ~]$ cut -d: -f1-5 /etc/passwd
root:x:0:0:root
bin:x:1:1:bin
daemon:x:2:2:daemon
adm:x:3:4:adm
lp:x:4:7:lp
sync:x:5:0:sync
shutdown:x:6:0:shutdown
halt:x:7:0:halt
mail:x:8:12:mail
operator:x:11:0:operator
games:x:12:100:games
ftp:x:14:50:FTP User
nobody:x:99:99:Nobody
ods:x:999:998:softhsm private keys owner
pegasus:x:66:65:tog-pegasus OpenPegasus WBEM/CIM services
systemd-network:x:192:192:systemd Network Management
dbus:x:81:81:System message bus
polkitd:x:998:996:User for polkitd
apache:x:48:48:Apache
tomcat:x:91:91:Apache Tomcat
colord:x:997:994:User for colord
```

- This command will show characters 1 to 3 and 8 to 12 from the emp.1st file:

```
$ cut -c1-3,8-12 /home/student/emp.1st
```

- The output of the date command is sent as an input to the cut command and only the first three characters are printed on screen, which is shown as follows:

```
$ date | cut -c1-3
Mon
```

The paste command

Using this utility, we can paste two files horizontally; for example, file_1 will become the first column and file_2 will become the second column:

```
$ paste file_1 file_2
```

The join command

Consider two files, namely `one.txt` and `two.txt`:

- The content of `one.txt` is as follows:

```
1 India
2 UK
3 Canada
4 US
5 Ireland
```

- The content of `two.txt` is as follows:

```
1 New Delhi
2 London
3 Toronto
4 Washington
5 Dublin
```

In this case, for both the files, the common fields are the fields that have serial numbers that are the same in both files. We can combine both files using the following command:

```
$ join one.txt two.txt
```

The output will be as follows:

```
1 India New Delhi
2 UK London
3 Canada Toronto
4 US Washington
5 Ireland Dublin
```

The uniq command

The following are a few examples showing the usage of the `uniq` command:

- This command removes duplicate adjacent lines from the file:

```
$ cat test
aa
aa
cc
cc
bb
bb
```

```
yy
zz
$ uniq test
```

- This output removes the duplicate adjacent lines from `test` file, shown as follows:

```
aa
cc
bb
yy
zz
```

- The next command only prints duplicate lines:

```
$ uniq -d test
```

- Output:

```
aa
cc
bb
```

- The following command prints the number of occurrences of all elements on an individual line:

```
$ uniq -c test
```

- Output:

```
2 aa
2 cc
2 bb
1 yy
1 zz
```

The comm command

The `comm` command shows the lines unique to `file_1` and `file_2` along with the common lines in them. We can use various options while using the command in the scripts:

```
$ cat file_1
Barack Obama
David Cameron
Narendra Modi
$ cat file_2
```

```
Barack Obama
Angela Markel
Vladimir Putin
$ comm --nocheck-order file_1 file_2
        Barack Obama
  David Cameron
      Engela Merkel
  Narendra Modi
        Vladimir Putin
```

In the preceding example, we can see the following:

- The first column shows the unique lines in `file_1`
- The second column shows the unique lines in `file_2`
- The last column shows the content common to both files

The output shows that the unique lines in `file_1` are `David Cameron` and `Narendra Modi`. The unique lines in the second file are `Engela Merkel` and `Vladimir Putin`. The common name in both the files is `Barack Obama`, which is displayed in the third column.

The tr command

The `tr` command is a Linux utility for text processing, such as translating, deleting, or squeezing repeated characters, which is shown as follows:

```
$ tr '[a-z]' '[A-Z]' < filename
```

This will translate the lowercase characters to uppercase:

```
$ tr '|' '~' < emp.lst
```

This will squeeze multiple spaces into a single space:

```
$ ls -l | tr -s " "
```

In this example, the `-s` option squeezes multiple contiguous occurrences of the character into a single char. Additionally, the `-d` option can remove characters.

The sort command

This command sorts the contents of a text file, line by line. The options are as follows:

- −n: Sorts as per the numeric value
- −d: Sorts as per the dictionary meaning
- −h: Compares as per the human-readable numbers (for example, 1K 2G)
- −r: Sorts in the reverse order
- −t: Option to specify a delimiter for fields
- +num: Specifies sort field numbers
- −knum: Specifies sort field numbers
- $ sort −k4 sample.txt: This will sort according to the fourth field

Sr	Examples of command usage	Explanation
1	sort sample.txt	Alphabetically sorts the lines
2	sort −u sample.txt	Duplicate entries are sorted
3	sort −r sample.txt	Reverse sort
4	sort −n −k3 sample.txt	Numerical sort of the third field

IO redirection

You will learn the very useful concept of I/O redirection in this section.

File descriptors

All I/O–including files, pipes, and sockets - are handled by the kernel via a mechanism called the **file descriptor**. A file descriptor is a small, unsigned integer, which is an index into a file-descriptor table maintained by the kernel, and used by the kernel to reference open files and I/O streams. Each process inherits its own file-descriptor table from its parent. The first three file descriptors are 0, 1, and 2. File descriptor 0 is standard input (stdin), 1 is standard output (stdout), and 2 is standard error (stderr). When you open a file, the next available descriptor is 3, and it will be assigned to the new file.

Redirection

When a file descriptor is assigned to something other than a terminal, this is called I/O redirection. The shell performs the redirection of output to a file by closing the standard output file descriptor 1 (the Terminal) and then assigning that descriptor to the file. When redirecting standard input, the shell closes file descriptor 0 (the Terminal) and assigns that descriptor to a file. The Bash shells handle errors by assigning a file to file descriptor 2. The following command will take input from the `sample.txt` file:

```
$ wc < sample.txt
```

The preceding command will take content from the `sample.text` file. The `wc` command will print the number of lines, words, and characters in the `sample.txt` file. This command will redirect output to be saved in the `log.txt` file:

```
$ echo "Hello world" > log.txt
```

This command will append the `Hello World` text to the `log.txt` file:

```
$ echo "Welcome to Shell Scripting" >> log.txt
```

The single > will overwrite or replace the existing text in the log file, and double >> will append the text to the log file. Let's see a few more examples:

```
$ tr '[A-Z]' '[a-z]' < sample.txt
```

The preceding `tr` command will read text from the `sample.txt` file. The `tr` command will convert all uppercase letters to lowercase letters and will print the converted text on screen:

```
$ ls > log.txt
$ cat log.txt
```

The output of the command is as follows:

```
dir_1
sample.txt
extra.file
```

In this example command, `ls` sends directory content to file `log.txt`. Whenever we want to store the result of the command in the file, we can use the preceding example.

```
$ date >> log.txt
$ cat log.txt
```

The output is as follows:

```
dir_1
dir_2
file_1
file_2
file_3
Sun Sept 17 12:57:22 PDT 2004
```

In the preceding example, we redirect and append the result of the date command to the log.txt file.

```
$ gcc hello.c 2> error_file
```

The gcc is a C language compiler program. If an error is encountered during compilation, then it will be redirected to error_file. The > character is used for a success result and 2> is used for error-result redirection. We can use error_file for debugging purposes:

```
$ find . -name "*.sh" > success_file 2> /dev/null
```

In the preceding example, we redirect output or success results to success_file, and errors to /dev/null. /dev/null is used to destroy the data, which we do not want to be shown on screen.

```
$ find . -name "*.sh" &> log.txt
```

The preceding command will redirect both output and errors to log.txt.

```
$ find . -name "*.sh"  > log.tx 2>&1
```

The preceding command will redirect the result to log.txt and send errors to where the output goes, such as log.txt.

```
$ echo "File needs an argument" 1>&2
```

The preceding command will send standard output to the standard error. This will merge the output with the standard errors. A summary of all I/O redirection commands is as follows:

< sample.txt	The command will take input from sample.txt
> sample.txt	The success result will be stored in sample.txt
>> sample.txt	The successive outputs will be appended to sample.txt
2> sample.txt	The error results will be stored in sample.txt
2>> sample.txt	The successive error outputs will be appended to sample.txt

`&> sample.txt`	This will store successes and errors, such as in `sample.txt`
`>& sample.txt`	This will store successes and errors, such as in `sample.txt` (the same as the previous example)
`2>&1`	This will redirect an error to where output goes
`1>&2`	This will redirect output to where errors go
`>|`	This overrides noclobber when redirecting the output
`<> filename`	This uses the file as both standard input and output if a device file (from `/dev`)
`cat xyz > success_file 2> error_file`	This stores success and failure in different files

The following is the summary of various meta-characters:

Char	Meaning	Example	Possible output
`*`	Matches with zero or multiple numbers of any character	`$ ls -l *.c file*`	`Sample.c, hello.c, file1, file_2, filebc`
`?`	Matches any single character	`$ ls -l file?`	`filea, fileb, file1`
`[..]`	Matches with any single character within the bracket	`$ ls -l file[abc]`	`filea, fileb, filec`
`;`	Command separator	`$cat filea; date`	Displays the content of `filea`, and displays the current date and time
`|`	Pipe between two commands	`$ cat filea	wc -l`	Prints the number of lines in `filea`
`()`	Groups commands; is used when the output of the command group has to be redirected	`$ (echo "***x.c***";cat x.c)>out`	Redirects the content of `x.c` with a heading `***x.c***` to the file out

Run the following command:

```
$ touch filea fileb filec fileab filebc filead filebd filead
$ touch file{1,2,3}
```

Try out the following command:

```
$ ls   s*
$ ls   file
$ ls   file[abc]
$ ls   file[abc][cd]
$ ls   file[^bc]
$ touch file file1 file2 file3 ... file20
$ ls ?????
file1
file2
file3
$ ls file*
file file1 file10 file2 file3
$ ls file[0-9]
file1 file2 file3
$ ls file[0-9]*
file1 file10 file2 file3
$ ls file[!1-2]
file3
```

Brace expansion

Curly braces allow you to specify a set of characters from which the shell automatically forms all possible combinations. To make this work, the characters to be combined with the given string must be specified as a comma-separated list with no spaces:

```
$ touch file{1,2,3}
$ ls
```

```
[student@localhost work]$ touch file{1,2,3}
[student@localhost work]$ ls
file1   file2   file3
[student@localhost work]$
```

```
$ mkdir directory{1,2,3}{a,b,c}
$ ls
```

```
[student@localhost work]$ mkdir directory{1,2,3}{a,b,c}
[student@localhost work]$ ls
directory1a  directory1c  directory2b  directory3a  directory3c
directory1b  directory2a  directory2c  directory3b
[student@localhost work]$
```

```
$ touch file{a..z}
$ ls
```

```
[student@localhost work]$ touch file{a..z}
[student@localhost work]$ ls
filea  filed  fileg  filej  filem  filep  files  filev  filey
fileb  filee  fileh  filek  filen  fileq  filet  filew  filez
filec  filef  filei  filel  fileo  filer  fileu  filex
[student@localhost work]$
```

The following is the summary of various I/O-redirection and logical operators:

Char	Meaning	Example	Possible Output
>	Output Redirection	$ ls > ls.out	Output of ls command is redirected(overwritten) to ls.out file
>>	Output Redirection (append)	$ ls >> ls.out	Output of ls command is redirected(appended) to ls.out file
<	Input Redirection	$ tr 'a' 'A' < file1	The tr command read input from file1 instead of keyboard(stdin)
`cmd` or $(cmd)	Command substitution	$echo `date` or $ echo $(date)	The command date is substituted with the result and sent to echo for display
||	OR Conditional Execution	$ test $x –gt 10 || $x –lt 15	Check whether x value is greater than 10 or less than 15
&&	AND Conditional Execution	$ test $x –gt 10 && $x –lt 15	Check whether x value is greater than 10 and less than 15

For example:

```
$ ls || echo "Command un-successful"
$ ls a abcd || echo "Command un-successful"
```

These commands will print Command un-successful if the ls command is unsuccessful.

Pattern matching with the vi editor

To learn about pattern matching, we will ensure that the pattern that we will search for is highlighted when the pattern searched for is found. The configuration file for vi is /etc/vimrc.In the vi editor, use the following commands for various options:

Sr.	Commands	Description
1	:set hlsearch	Highlights the search pattern
2	:se[t] showmode	Shows when you are in insert mode
3	:se[t] ic	Ignores case when searching
4	:set noic	Shows a case-sensitive search

The user should open the file in vi, press the *Esc* button so that it enters command mode, and then type colon, followed by these commands. The following are the commands for pattern search and replace:

Sr.	Commands	Description
1	/pat	This searches for the pattern pat and places the cursor where the pattern occurs
2	/	This repeats the last search
3	:%s/old/new/g	Globally, all the occurrences of old will be replaced by new
4	:#,#s/old/new/g	#,# should be replaced with the numbers of the two lines (say between line numbers 3 and 6), for example, 3,6s/am/was/g

The following is an example of a regular expression for replacing Tom with David:

```
:1,$s/tom/David/g              // from line 1 to end ($), replace tom by
David
:1,$s/<[tT]om>/David/g   // start and end of word   <   >
```

This is another example of a regular expression. Create the `love.txt` file, as follows:

```
Man has love for Art
World is full of love
Love makes world wonderful
love looove lve
love
Love love lover loves
I like "Unix" more than DOS
I love "Unix"/
I said I love "Unix"
I love "unix" a lot
```

Use the following commands for testing pattern-searching facilities:

Command	Description
`:set hlsearch`	This will highlight the search pattern, when it is found
`/love/`	This will highlight any text matching with `love`. Use n for forward and N for backward in the next search
`/^love/`	This will highlight the line starting with `love`
`/love$/`	This will highlight the line ending with `love`
`/^love$/`	This will highlight a line containing only the word `love`
`/l.ve/`	This will highlight any character match for `.`
`/o*ve/`	This will highlight `love`, `loooove`, and `lve`
`/[Ll]ove/`	This will search for patterns Love and love
`/ove[a-z]/`	This will highlight any matching character in the a to z range
`/ove[^a-zA-Z0-9" "]/`	Except for alpha-numeric characters, this will match punctuation marks such as , ; : and similar
`:%s/unix/Linux/g`	This will replace `unix` with `Linux`
`:1,$s/unix/Linux/g`	This will replace `unix` with `Linux` from line 1 to the end ($)
`:1,$s/<[uU]nix>/Linux/g`	This will start and end of word < >
`/^[A-Z]..$/`	This will highlight a line starting with an uppercase letter, two chars and then end of line
`/^[A-Z][a-z ]*3[0-5]/`	This will highlight any line ending with 30 to 35
`/[a-z]* ./`	This will highlight any line with lowercase and ending with `.`

Pattern searching using grep

The command `g/RE/p` stands for globally search for the regular expression (RE) and print the line. The return statuses are `0` for success, `1` for pattern not found, and `2` for file not found:

```
$ ps -ef | grep root
```

The preceding command will show all processes running currently whose user ID is `root`.

```
$ ll /proc | grep "cpuinfo"
```

The preceding command will show the file with the name `cpuinfo` from the `/proc` directory.

```
$ grep -lir "text" *         // show only file names containing text
//
$ grep -ir "text" dir_name   // show lines of files //
```

We will try the following commands on file `love.txt`:

Meta-character	Function	Example	Description
^	Beginning-of-line anchor	`'^mango'`	Will display all lines beginning with `mango`
$	End-of-line anchor	`'mango'$'`	Will display all lines ending with `mango`
.	Matches a single character	`'m..o'`	Will display lines containing m, followed by two characters, followed by an o
*	Matches zero or more characters preceding the asterisk	`'*mango'`	Will display lines with zero or more spaces, followed by the pattern `mango`
[ ]	Matches a single character in the set	`'[Mm]ango'`	Will display lines containing `Mango` or `mango`
[^]	Matches a single character not in the set	`'[^A-M]ango'`	Will display lines not containing a character in the range A through M, followed by `ango`
<	Beginning-of-word anchor	`'<mango'`	Will display lines containing a word that begins with `mango`
>	End-of-word anchor	`'mango>'`	Will display lines containing a word that ends with `mango`

We will create a new file `sample.txt`, as follows:

```
Apple Fruit 5   4.5

Potato Vegetable 4   .5

Onion Vegetable .3   8

Guava Fruit 5   1.5

Almonds Nuts 1 16

Tomato Vegetable 3   6

Cashew Nuts 2   12

Mango Fruit 6   6

Watermelon Fruit 5   1
```

We will try the following commands on the `sample.txt` file:

Sr. no.	Command	Description
1	grep Fruit sample.txt	This will show all lines with pattern Fruit
2	grep Fruit G*	This searches for pattern Fruit in all files starting with G
3	grep '^M' sample.txt	This searches for all lines starting with M
4	grep '6$' sample.txt	This searches for lines ending with 6
5	grep '1..' sample.txt	This displays lines containing 1 and any character after it
6	grep '.6' sample.txt	This shows lines containing 6
7	grep '^[AT]' sample.txt	This searches for lines starting with A or T
8	grep '[^0-9]' sample.txt	This searches for lines that contain at least one alphabetic character
9	grep '[A-Z][A-Z] [A-Z]' sample.txt	This searches for word containing an uppercase letter, uppercase letter, space, and uppercase letter
10	grep '[a-z]{8}' sample.txt	This displays all lines in which there are at least eight consecutive lowercase letters
11	grep '<Fruit' sample.txt	This displays all lines containing a word starting with Fruit. The < is the beginning-of-word anchor

12	`grep '<Fruit>' sample.txt`	This displays the line if it contains the word `Fruit`. The `<` is the beginning-of-word anchor and the `>` is the end-of-word anchor
13	`grep '<[A-Z].*o>' sample.txt`	This displays all lines containing a word starting with an uppercase letter, followed by any number of characters and ending in `o`
14	`grep -n '^south' sample.txt`	This displays line numbers also
15	`grep -i 'pat' sample.txt`	This displays the results of a case-insensitive search
16	`grep -v 'Onion' sample.txt > tempmv temp sample.txt`	This deletes the line containing the pattern
17	`grep -l 'Nuts' *`	This lists files containing the pattern
18	`grep -c 'Nuts' sample.txt`	This prints the number of lines where the pattern is present
19	`grep -w 'Nuts' sample.txt`	This counts where the whole world pattern is present, not as a part of a word

Summary

In this chapter, you have learned about using the `more`, `less`, `head`, and `tail` commands, and text processing tools such as `cut`, `paste`, `comm`, and `uniq`. You also have learned what standard input, standard output, and standard errors are. Finally, you have learned about meta-characters, and pattern matching using vi and grep. In the next chapter, you will learn about analysing the shell interpretation of commands, and you will learn about working with command substitution, command separators, and pipes.

4
Working with Commands

In the last chapter, you learned about using `more`, `less`, `head`, and `tail` commands, and text processing tools such as `diff`, `cut`, `paste`, `comm`, and `uniq`. You learned what standard input, output, and standard error are. You also learned about metacharacters and pattern matching using vi and `grep`.

In this chapter, you will learn the following topics:

- Learning shell interpretation of commands
- Working with command substitution
- Working with command separators
- Working with pipes

Learning shell interpretation of commands

When we log in, the $ sign will be visible in the shell Terminal (# prompt if you are logged in as the root or administrator). The Bash shell runs scripts as the interpreter. Whenever we type a command, the Bash shell will read them as a series of words (tokens). Each word is separated by a space ( ), semicolon (;), or any other command delimiter. We terminate the command by pressing the *Enter* key. This will insert a newline character at the end of the command. The first word is taken as a command, then consecutive words are treated as options or parameters.

The shell processes the command line as follows:

- If applicable, the substitution of history commands
- Converting the command line into tokens and words
- Updating the history
- Processing quotes

- Defining functions and substitution of aliases
- Setting up of pipes, redirection, and background
- Substitution of variables (such as $name and $user) is performed
- Command substitution (echocal and echodate) is performed
- Globing is performed (filename substitution, such as ls *)
- Execution of the command

The sequence of execution of different types of commands will be as follows:

- Aliases (l, ll, egrep, and similar)
- Keywords (for, if, while, and similar)
- Functions (user-defined or shell-defined functions)
- The builtin commands (bg, fg, source, cd, and similar)
- Executable external commands and scripts (command from the bin and sbin folder)

Whenever a command is typed in a shell or terminal, the complete command will be tokenized, and then shell will check if the command is an alias.

Aliases, keywords, functions, and builtin commands are executed in the current shell and, therefore their execution is fast compared to executable external commands or scripts. Executable external commands will have a corresponding binary file or shell script file in the file system, which will be stored in any folder. The shell will search for the binary file or script of a command by searching in the PATH environment variable. If we want to know what type of command it is, such as if it is an alias, a function, or internal command, it can be found out by the type builtin command, which is shown as follows:

```
$ type mkdir
mkdir is /usr/bin/mkdir
$ type cd
cd is a shell builtin
$ type ll
ll is aliased to `ls -l --color=auto'
$ type hello
hello is a function
hello ()
{
        echo "Hello World !";
}
$ type for
for is a shell keyword
```

Checking and disabling shell internal commands

Bash provides a few `builtin` commands to change the sequence of command-line processing. We can use these `builtin` commands to change the default behaviour of command-line processing.

- The `builtin` command will disable aliases and functions for the command that follows the command. The shell will search for the external command and the `builtin` command will search for the command passed as an argument, as follows:

`$ command ls`

- This will facilitate the ignoring of aliases and functions and the external `ls` command will execute.

- The `builtin` command will work as follows:

`$ builtin BUILT-IN`

- This will ignore aliases and functions from the shell environment and only `builtin` commands and external commands will be processed.

- The `break builtin` command will work as follows:

`$ builtin -n break`

- This will disable the `builtin` break and the external `break` command will be processed.

- To display all shell `builtin` commands, give the command as follows:

`$ enable`

- The output on the screen will show the following as shell internal commands:

.	command	eval	history	pwd	test
..	compgen	exec	jobs	read	times
[	complete	exit	kill	readarray	trap
alias	compopt	export	let	readonly	true
bg	continue	false	local	return	type
bind	declare	fc	logout	set, unset	typeset

```
break    dirs    fg       mapfile shift    ulimit
builtin disown  getopts popd     shopt    umask
caller  echo    hash     printf  source   unalias
cd      enable  help     pushd   suspend  wait
```

- The shell `builtin` command can be disabled as follows:

```
$ enable -n built-in-command
```

- For example: `$ enable -n test`
- In this case, in my shell, if we have to test an external command, then, instead of the internal `test` command, the external `test` command will be executed.

The exit status

In shell scripting, we need to check if the last command has successfully executed or not, for example, whether a file or directory is present or not. As per the result, our shell script will continue processing.

For this purpose, the bash shell has one status variable ?. The status of the last command execution is stored in ?. The range of numerical values stored in ? will be from 0 to 255. If successful in execution, then the value will be 0; otherwise, it will be non-zero, which is as follows:

```
$ ls
$ echo $?
0
```

Here, zero as the return value indicates success.

In the next case, we see the following:

```
$ ls /root
ls: cannot open directory /root: Permission denied
$ echo $?
2
```

Here, a non-zero value indicates an error in the last command execution.

In the next case, we see:

```
$ find / -name hello.c
$ echo $?
```

The return value will indicate if the `hello.c` file is present or not!

Command substitution

On a keyboard, there is one interesting key, the backward quote, `` ` ``. This key is normally situated below the Esc key. If we place text between two successive backquotes, then `echo` will execute those as commands instead of processing them as plain text.

Alternate syntax for `$(command)` is the backtick character `` ` ``, which we can see as follows:

```
$(command) or `command`
```

For example:

- We need to use proper double quotes, as follows:

```
$ echo "Hello, whoami"
```

- The next command will print the text as it is; such as `Hello, whoami`:

```
Hello, whoami
```

- Use proper double quotes and single backquotes:

```
$ echo "Hello, `whoami`."
Hello, student
```

- When we enclose `whoami` text in the `` ` `` characters, the same text that was printed as plain text will run as a command, and command output will be printed on the screen.

- Use proper double quotes:

```
$ echo "Hello, $(whoami)."
Hello, student.
```

- This is the same as earlier.

Another example:

```
echo "Today is date"
```

Output:

```
Today is date
```

A similar example:

```
/
```

Another example is:

```
echo "Today is $(date)"
```

The output is:

```
Today is Fri Mar 20 15:55:58 IST 2015
```

Furthermore, similar examples include:

```
$ echo $(cal)
```

```
[student@localhost ~]$ echo $(cal)
January 2018 Su Mo Tu We Th Fr Sa 1 2 3 4 5 6 7 8 9 10 11 12 13 14 15 16 17 18
19 20 21 22 23 24 25 26 27 28 29 30 31
```

In this example, new lines are lost.

Another example includes:

```
$ echo "$(cal)"
```

```
[student@localhost ~]$ echo "$(cal)"
      January 2018
Su Mo Tu We Th Fr Sa
    1  2  3  4  5  6
 7  8  9 10 11 12 13
14 15 16 17 18 19 20
21 22 23 24 25 26 27
28 29 30 31
```

Here, the display is properly formatted.

Next, the nesting of commands is as follows:

```
$ pwd
/home/student/work
$ dirname="$(basename $(pwd)) "
$ echo $dirname
```

```
[student@localhost ~]$ pwd
/home/student
[student@localhost ~]$
[student@localhost ~]$ dirname="$(basename $(pwd)) "
[student@localhost ~]$
[student@localhost ~]$ echo $dirname
student
```

This command shows us that the base directory for the current directory is student.

Command separators

Commands can also be combined in such a way that they are executed in a particular sequence.

Command1; command2

A command line can consist of multiple commands. Each command is separated by a semicolon, and the command line is terminated with a newline. The exit status is that of the last command in the chain of commands.

The first command is executed, and the second one is started as soon as the first one has finished:

```
$ w; date
```

Output:

```
[student@localhost ~]$ w; date
 16:02:27 up  1:53,  2 users,  load average: 0.01, 0.03, 0.05
USER     TTY      FROM             LOGIN@   IDLE   JCPU   PCPU WHAT
student  :0       :0               14:09    ?xdm?  1:04   0.22s /usr/libexec/gn
student  pts/0    :0               16:00    3.00s  0.05s  0.02s w
Thu Jan  4 16:02:27 IST 2018
```

```
$ w ; date > whoandwhen
```

Output from the `date` command will be redirected to the `whoandwhen` file.

In the preceding example, we can see that when we put multiple commands on the same line, but separated by the `;` command, then those commands execute sequentially one by one:

```
$ date; who am i
Tue Mar 10 23:21:38 PDT 201
student  pts/0          2015-03-10 23:12 (:0.0)
```

In the preceding example, the `date` command is executed first and the `who am I` command will be executed next. Both the commands are typed on the same lines, separated by the `;` command.

Command grouping

Commands may also be grouped so that all of the output is either piped to another command or redirected to a file:

```
$ ( ls; pwd; date ) > outputfile
```

The output of each of the commands is sent to the file, `outputfile`. The spaces inside the parentheses are necessary:

```
$ ( w ; date ) > whoandwhen
```

The output of the `w` command and `date` will be redirected to the `whoandwhen` file:

```
$ (echo "***x.c***";cat x.c) > log.txt
```

Output:

This redirects the content of `x.c` with a heading `***x.c***` to the file out:

```
$ (pwd; ls; date) > log.txt
```

Output:

This redirects the output of commands `pwd`, `ls`, and `date` in the `log.txt` file.

Logical operators

Let's now take a look at logical operators.

Command1 & command2

The first command is started in the background to continue until it has finished; immediately after starting the first command, the second command is started and it will run in the foreground:

```
$ find / -name "*.z" & ls
---------------      -----
Command1             command2
```

In the preceding example, the first command, find, will start running in the background and, while the find command is running in the background, the ls command will start running in the foreground.

Command1 && command2

The second command is only started if the first command is successful. To achieve this, the shell checks the exit (return) status of the first command and starts the second command only if and when that exit status is found to be 0:

```
$ ls /home/ganesh && echo "Command executed successfully"
Since we are working as user ganesh,
$ ls /root   && echo "Command executed successfully"
```

Since we are working as a normal user, we cannot access the /root directory. Therefore, nothing will be printed on screen.

Command1 || command2

The second command is only started if the first command fails. The shell checks the exit status of the first command and starts the second command only if that exit status is not equal to 0:

```
$ ls /root  ||  echo "Command execution failed"
```

Example:

```
$ ls || echo "command ls failed"
```

In the preceding example, if `ls` runs successfully, then `echo` will not be called. If the `ls` command fails, such as `$ ls /root`, and if the user is not the root, then `ls` will fail and the `echo` command will print `command ls failed`.

When `&&` or `||` are used, the exit status of the first command is checked first, and then the decision to perform the next will be taken.

For example:

```
$ ls
$ echo $?
0
$ ls /root
    ls: /root: Permission denied
$ echo $?
1
$ tar cvzf /dev/st0 /home /etc || mail -s "Something went wrong with
the backup" root
```

If we give the command as follows:

```
$ cd /home/student/work/temp/; rm -rf *
```

Initially, the shell will change to the `/home/student/work/temp` folder, and then it will delete all files and folders.

If we enter the command as follows:

```
cd /backup/ol/home/student/work/temp/ && rm * -rf
```

This will first change to the required folder, and then the `rm` command will be called for deletion. The problem with `;` is that even if the shell fails to change to the required folder, the `rm` command will execute and it will delete all the files and folders from your original folder. This will be really dangerous.

For example:

```
$ [[ "a" = "b" ]]; echo ok
ok
```

In this case, the `[[ ]]` expression will evaluate to false. Since the semicolon will not check the status of the earlier command, `ok` will be printed even if the first `[[ ]]` expression fails.

```
$ [[ "a" = "b" ]] && echo ok
```

In this case, the `[[ ]]` expression will evaluate to false. As the first expression is false, the "`&&`" operator will not proceed to execute the next command.

In this case, `ok` will be printed only if `[[ ]]` is true.

Pipes

We have already used pipes in many earlier sections. It is a tool for inter-process communication:

```
$ command_1 | command_2
```

In this case, the output of `command_1` will be sent as an input to `command_2`. The limitation is that the communication is half duplex. This means the data can flow in only one direction. Normally, for inter-process communication, you need to open files and then get the file descriptor. This will be used to write to the pipe file. Again, we need to create a `Fifo` file with special commands. The preceding technique simplifies this process. We only need to insert `|` in between the two processes. The operating system creates one intermediate buffer. This buffer is used for storing the data from one command and will be used again for the second command.

A simple example is as follows:

```
$ who | wc
```

The preceding simple command will carry out three different activities. First, it will copy the output of the `who` command to the temporary file. Then the `wc` command will read the temporary file and display the result. Finally, the temporary file will be deleted.

Normally, there will be two processes. The first command is the writer process. The second process is the reader process. The writer process will write to `temp_file` and the reader will read from `temp_file`. Examples of writer processes are `ps`, `ls`, and `date`. Examples of reader processes are `wc`, `cat`, `grep`, and `sort`.

Summary

In this chapter, you learned about how the shell interprets any command entered on the command line. We also studied command substitution and separators in detail.

In the next chapter, you will learn about variables and environment variables. You will also learn about how to export environment variables, and then you will learn about read-only variables, command-line arguments, and arrays.

5
Exploring Expressions and Variables

In the last chapter, you learned about how shell interprets any command that is entered into the Terminal or the command line. We also studied command substitution and separators in detail.

In this chapter, we will cover following topics:

- Working with environment variables
- Exporting variables
- Working with read-only variables
- Working with command-line arguments (special variables, `set` and `shift`, and `getopt`)
- Working with arrays

Understanding variables

Let's learn about creating variables in a shell.

Declaring variables in Linux is very easy. We just need to use the variable name and initialize it with the required content.

```
$ person="Ganesh Naik"
```

To get the content of the variable, we need to add the prefix $ before the variable, for example:

```
$ echo person
person
$ echo $person
Ganesh Naik
```

The `unset` command can be used to delete the declared variable:

```
$ a=20$ echo $a$ unset a
```

The `unset` command will clear or remove the variable from the shell environment as well.

Here, the `set` command will show all variables declared in the shell:

```
$ person="Ganesh Naik"$ echo $person$ set
```

Here, using the `declare` command with the −x option will make it an environmental or global variable. We will find out more about environmental variables in the next section.

$ declare -x variable=value

Here, the `env` command will display all environmental variables:

```
$ env
```

Whenever we declare a `variable`, that `variable` will be available in the current Terminal or shell. This `variable` will not be available to any other Terminal or shell:

```
variable=value
```

Let's write a shell script, as follows:

```
#!/bin/bash
# This script clears the window, greets the user,
# and displays the current date and time.

clear                               # Clear the window
echo "SCRIPT BEGINS"
echo "Hello $LOGNAME!"              # Greet the user
echo

echo "Today's date and time:"
date                                # Display current date and time
echo                   # Will print empty line
```

```
my_num=50
my_day="Sunday"

echo "The value of my_num is $my_num"
echo "The value of my_day is $my_day"
echo

echo "SCRIPT FINISHED!!"
echo
```

Let's see the effect of $, "", ' ' on variable behavior:

```
#!/bin/bash

planet="Earth"

echo $planet
echo "$planet"
echo '$planet'
echo $planet

exit 0
```

The output is as follows:

```
Earth
Earth
$planet
$planet
```

From the preceding script's execution, we can observe that `$variable` and `"$ variable"` can be used to display the content of the variable. But if we use `'$variable'` or `$variable`, then the special functionality of the $ symbol is not available. The $ symbol is used as a simple text character instead of utilizing its special functionality of getting the variable's content.

Working with environment variables

Environmental variables are inherited by any subshells or child processes, for example, `HOME`, `PATH`. Every shell Terminal has a memory area called the environment. Shell keeps all details and settings in the environment. When we start a new Terminal or shell, this environment is created every time.

We can view the environment variables with the following command:

```
$ env
```

Or we can use this:

```
$ printenv
```

The output of the $ env command is as follows:

```
[student@localhost ~]$
[student@localhost ~]$ env
XDG_VTNR=1
SSH_AGENT_PID=2399
XDG_SESSION_ID=2
HOSTNAME=localhost.localdomain
IMSETTINGS_INTEGRATE_DESKTOP=yes
TERM=xterm-256color
SHELL=/bin/bash
XDG_MENU_PREFIX=gnome-
VTE_VERSION=4602
HISTSIZE=1000
PERL5LIB=/home/student/perl5/lib/perl5:
GJS_DEBUG_OUTPUT=stderr
WINDOWID=35651590
QTDIR=/usr/lib64/qt-3.3
QTINC=/usr/lib64/qt-3.3/include
GJS_DEBUG_TOPICS=JS ERROR;JS LOG
PERL_MB_OPT=--install_base /home/student/perl5
IMSETTINGS_MODULE=none
QT_GRAPHICSSYSTEM_CHECKED=1
USER=student
LS_COLORS=rs=0:di=38;5;27:ln=38;5;51:mh=44;38;5;15:pi=40;38;5;11:so=38;5;13:do=3
```

The list of environment variables will be quite extensive. I advise you to browse through the complete list. We can change the content of any of these environment variables.

Environmental variables are defined in a Terminal or shell. They will be available in any subshells or child shells created from the current shell Terminal. You will learn about these activities in the next few sections. You have already learned that every command in a shell creates a new subshell from the current shell.

The following is a brief summary of a few environmental variables:

Variable Description

Variable	Description
HOME	The user's home directory
PATH	The search path for commands
PWD	Current working directory
IFS	The internal field separator; that is, the character that separates individual arguments from one another
PS1	The primary shell prompt
PS2	The secondary shell prompt
PS3	The tertiary shell prompt (see select)
?	The exit status or (return value) of the most recent child process
$	The process ID of the current shell itself
#	The number of arguments passed to the shell
0-9	Argument 0 (usually the command itself), argument 1, and so on, as passed to the shell
*	All arguments (with the exception of argument 0) as separate words or arguments
@	All arguments (with the exception of argument 0) as separate words or arguments

Whenever any user logs in, the /etc/profile shell script is executed.

For every user, the .bash_profile Shell script is stored in the home folder. The complete path or location is /home/user_name/.profile.

Whenever a new Terminal is created, every new Terminal will execute script .bashrc, which is located in the home folder of every user.

The local variable and its scope

In the current shell, we can create and store user-defined variables. These may contain characters, digits, and _. A variable should not start with a digit. Normally, for environment variables, uppercase characters are used.

If we create a new variable, it will not be available in the subshells. The newly created variable will be available only in the current shell. If we run a Shell script, then the local variables will not be available in the commands called by the Shell script. Shell has one special variable, $$. This variable contains the process ID of the current shell.

Let's try a few commands:

This is the process ID of the current shell:

```
$ echo $$1234
```

We declare the variable name and initialize it:

```
$ name="Ganesh Naik"$ echo $nameGanesh Naik
```

This command will create a new subshell:

```
$ bash
```

This is the process ID of the newly created subshell:

```
$ echo $$1678
```

From the following, nothing will be displayed, as the local variables from the parent shell are not inherited in the newly created child shell or subshell:

```
$ echo $name
```

We will exit the subshell and return to the original shell Terminal:

```
$ exit
```

This is the process ID of the current shell or parent shell:

```
$ echo $$1234
```

This displays the presence of the variable in the original shell or parent shell:

```
$ echo $nameGanesh Naik
```

Variables created in the current shell will not be available in a subshell or child shell. If we need to use a variable in a child shell as well, then we need to export it using the export command.

Exporting variables

We can use the export command to make variables available in the child process or subshell. But if we declare new variables in the child process and export it in the child process, the variable will not be available in parent process. The parent process can export variables to a child, but the child process cannot export variables to the parent process.

Whenever we create a Shell script and execute it, a new shell process is created and the Shell script runs in that process. Any exported variable values are available to the new shell or to any sub-process.

We can export any variable as follows:

```
$ export NAME
```

Or we can use this:

```
$ declare -x NAME
```

Let's try to understand the concept of exporting the variable, using the following example:

```
$ PERSON="Ganesh Naik"$ export PERSON$ echo $PERSONGanesh Naik$ echo $$515
```

The process ID of the current shell or parent shell is 515.

This will start a subshell:

```
$ bash
```

This is the process ID of new or sub-shell:

```
$ echo $$526
```

Let us check the presence of variables:

```
$ echo $PERSONGanesh Naik$ PERSON="Author"$ echo $PERSONAuthor$ exit
```

This will terminate the subshell, and it will be placed in the parent shell:

```
$ echo $$
515
```

This displays the presence of the variable in the original shell or parent shell:

```
$ echo $PERSONGanesh Naik
```

Let's write a shell script to use the concept we have learned:

```
# Ubuntu Timezone files location : /usr/share/zoneinfo/
# redhat "/etc/localtime"  instead of "/etc/timezone"
# In Redhat
# ln -sf /usr/share/zoneinfo/America/Los_Angeles /etc/localtime

export TZ=America/Los_Angeles
echo "Your Timezone is = $TZ"
date
export TZ=Asia/Tokyo
echo "Your Timezone is = $TZ"
date

unset TZ

echo "Your Timezone is = $(cat /etc/timezone)"
# For Redhat or Fedora /etc/localtime
date
```

```
Your Timezone is = America/Los_Angeles
Thu Jan  4 21:06:59 PST 2018
Your Timezone is = Asia/Tokyo
Fri Jan  5 14:06:59 JST 2018
cat: /etc/timezone: No such file or directory
Your Timezone is =
Fri Jan  5 10:36:59 IST 2018
```

The date command checks the TZ environmental variable. We initialized the TZ for Los_Angeles, then to Tokyo, and, finally, we removed it. We can see the difference in the date command output.

Let's write another Shell script to study the parent and child process, and the export of variables.

Create the export1.sh shell script:

```
#!/bin/bash
foo="The first variable foo"
export bar="The second variable bar"
./export2.sh

Create another shell script export2.sh
```

```
#!/bin/bash
echo "$foo"
echo "$bar"
```

```
[student@localhost work]$
[student@localhost work]$ ./export1.sh

The second variable bar
[student@localhost work]$
```

The shell script `export1.sh` runs as a parent process and `export2.sh` is started as a child process of `export1.sh`. We can clearly see that variable `bar`, which was exported, is available in the child process, but the variable `foo`, which was not exported, is not available in the child process.

Working with read-only variables

During shell scripting, we may need a few variables, which cannot be modified. This may be needed for security reasons. We can declare variables as read-only by using the following read-only command:

```
$ readonly currency=Dollars
```

Let's try to remove the variable:

```
$ unset currencybash: unset: currency: cannot unset: readonly variable
```

If we try to change or remove the read-only variable in the script, it will give the following error:

```
#!/bin/bash
AUTHOR="Ganesh Naik"
readonly AUTHOR
AUTHOR="John"
```

This will produce the following result:

```
/bin/sh: AUTHOR: This variable is read only.
```

Another technique is as follows:

```
declare -r variable=1
echo "variable=$variable"
(( var1++ ))
```

The output after execution of the script is this:

```
line 4: variable: readonly variable
```

Working with command-line arguments (special variables, set and shift, getopt)

Command-line arguments are required for the following reasons:

- They inform the utility, or they command which file or group of files to process (reading/writing of files)
- Command-line arguments tell the command/utility which option to use

Check out the following command line:

```
[student@localhost ~]$ my_program  arg1  arg2  arg3
```

If `my_command` is a bash shell script, then we can access every command-line positional parameter inside the script, as follows:

```
$0 would contain "my_program"      # Command
$1 would contain "arg1"            # First parameter
$2 would contain "arg2"            # Second parameter
$3 would contain "arg3"            # Third parameter
```

The following is a summary of the positional parameters:

`$0`   Shell-script name or command

`$1-$9` Positional parameters 1-9

`${10}` Positional parameter 10

`$#`   Total number of parameters

`$*`   Evaluates for all the positional parameters

`$@`   Same as `$*`, except when double quoted

`"$*"`   Displays all parameters as `"$1 $2 $3"`, and so on

`"$@"`   Displays all parameters as `"$1" "$2" "$3"`, and so on

Let's create a script `parameter.sh`, as follows:

```
#!/bin/bash
echo "Total number of parameters are = $#"
echo "Script name = $0"
echo "First Parameter is $1"
echo "Second Parameter is $2"
echo "Third Parameter is $3"
echo "Fourth Parameter is $4"
echo "Fifth Parameter is $5"
echo "All parameters are = $*"
```

Then, as usual, give execute permission to the script and then execute it:

```
./parameter.sh London Washington Delhi Dhaka Paris
```

The output is as follows:

```
Total number of parameters are = 5Command is = ./parameter.shFirst
Parameter is LondonSecond Parameter is WashingtonThird Parameter is
DelhiFourth Parameter is DhakaFifth Parameter is ParisAll parameters are =
London Washington Delhi Dhaka Paris
```

Understanding set

Many times, we may not pass arguments to the command line, but we may need to set parameters internally inside the script.

We can declare parameters with the `set` command, as follows:

```
$ set USA Canada UK France$ echo $1USA$ echo $2Canada$ echo $3UK$ echo
$4France
```

We can use this inside the `set_01.sh` script, as follows:

```
#!/bin/bash
set USA Canada UK France
echo $1
echo $2
echo $3
echo $4
```

Run the script as this:

```
$ ./set.sh
```

The output is as follows:

USACanadaUKFrance

Following is a summary of the declare options:

Option	Meaning
-a	An array is created
-f	Displays the function names and definitions
-F	Displays only the function names
-i	Makes the variables integer types
-r	Makes the variables read-only
-x	Exports the variables

Type in the following commands:

```
set One Two Three Four Five
echo $0      # This will show command
echo $1       # This will show first parameter
echo $2echo $*   # This will list all parameters
echo $#    # This will list total number of parameters
echo ${10} ${11}  # Use this syntax for parameters for 10th and           #
11th parameters
```

Let's write script set_02.sh, as follows:

```
#!/bin/bash
echo The date is $(date)
set $(date)
echo The month is $2
exit 0
```

The output is as follows:

```
[student@localhost work]$ bash set_03.sh
Executing script set_03.sh

One two three in German are:
eins
zwei
drei
name phone address birthdate salary
At this time $1 =  name and $4 =  birthdate
```

In the script $ (date), the command will execute, and the output of that command will be used as $1, $2, $3, and so on. We have used $2 to extract the month from the output.

Let's write script set_03.sh, as follows:

```bash
#!/bin/bash

echo "Executing script $0"
echo $1 $2 $3

set eins zwei drei
echo "One two three in German are:"
echo "$1"
echo "$2"
echo "$3"

textline="name phone address birthdate salary"
set $textline
echo "$*"
echo 'At this time $1 = '$1' and $4 = '$4''
```

The output is as follows:

```
Executing script ./hello.sh

One two three in German are:
eins
zwei
drei

name phone address birthdate salary
At this time $1 = name and $4 = birthdate
```

```
[student@localhost work]$ bash shift_02.sh 1 2 3 4 5 6 7 8 9 10 11 12 13
$#:   13
$@:   1 2 3 4 5 6 7 8 9 10 11 12 13
$*:   1 2 3 4 5 6 7 8 9 10 11 12 13

$1 $2 $9 $10 are:  1 2 9 10

$#:   12
$@:   2 3 4 5 6 7 8 9 10 11 12 13
$*:   2 3 4 5 6 7 8 9 10 11 12 13

$1 $2 $9 are:  2 3 10
$#:   10
$@:   4 5 6 7 8 9 10 11 12 13
$*:   4 5 6 7 8 9 10 11 12 13

$1 $2 $9 are:  4 5 12
${10}:   13
```

In this script, the output shows:

1. Initially, when the set is not called, then $1, $2, and $3 do not contain any information.
2. Then, we set $1 to $3 as GERMAN numerals in words.
3. Then, we set $1 to $5 as the name, phone number, address, date of birth, and salary, respectively.

Understanding shift

Using shift, we can change the parameter to which $1 and $2 are pointing to the next variable.

Create script shift_01.sh, as follows:

```
#!/bin/bash
echo "All Arguments Passed are as follow : "
echo $*
echo "Shift By one Position :"
shift
echo "Value of Positional Parameter $ 1 after shift :"
echo $1
echo "Shift by Two Positions :"
shift 2
echo "Value of Positional Parameter $ 1 After two Shifts :"
echo $1
```

Execute the following command:

```
$ chmod +x shift_01.sh$ ./shift_01.sh One Two Three Four
```

The output is as follows:

```
[student@localhost ~]$ ./shift_01.sh One Two Three Four
All arguments passed are as follows:
One Two Three Four
Shift by one position.
Here, the value of the positional parameter $1 after shift is:
Two
Shift by two positions.
The value of the positional parameter $1 after two shifts:
Four
```

We can see that, initially, $1 was One. After the shift, $1 will be pointing to Two. Once the shift has been done, the value in position 1 is always destroyed and is inaccessible.

Create script `shift_02.sh`, as follows:

```bash
#!/bin/bash

echo '$#: ' $#
echo '$@: ' $@
echo '$*: ' $*
echo
echo '$1 $2 $9 $10 are: ' $1 $2 $9 $10
echo

shift
echo '$#: ' $#
echo '$@: ' $@
echo '$*: ' $*
echo
echo '$1 $2 $9 are: ' $1 $2 $9

shift 2
echo '$#: ' $#
echo '$@: ' $@
echo '$*: ' $*
echo
echo '$1 $2 $9 are: ' $1 $2 $9

echo '${10}: ' ${10}
```

```
[student@localhost work]$ bash shift_02.sh 1 2 3 4 5 6 7 8 9 10 11 12 13
$#:   13
$@:   1 2 3 4 5 6 7 8 9 10 11 12 13
$*:   1 2 3 4 5 6 7 8 9 10 11 12 13

$1 $2 $9 $10 are:  1 2 9 10

$#:   12
$@:   2 3 4 5 6 7 8 9 10 11 12 13
$*:   2 3 4 5 6 7 8 9 10 11 12 13

$1 $2 $9 are:  2 3 10
$#:   10
$@:   4 5 6 7 8 9 10 11 12 13
$*:   4 5 6 7 8 9 10 11 12 13

$1 $2 $9 are:  4 5 12
${10}:  13
```

From this script's execution, the following output is shown:

1. Initially, $1 to $13 were numerical values 1 to 13, respectively.
2. When we called the command shift, it then$1 shifted to number 2, and all $numbers were shifted accordingly.
3. When we called the command shift 2, then $1 shifted to number 4 and all $numbers were shifted accordingly.

Resetting positional parameters

In certain situations, we may need to reset original positional parameters.

Let's try the following:

```
$ set Alan John Dennis
```

This will reset the positional parameters.

Now $1 is Alan, $2 is John, and $3 is Dennis.

Inside scripts, we can save positional parameters in a variable, as follows:

```
oldargs=$*
```

Then, we can set new positional parameters.

In addition, we can bring back our original positional parameters, as follows:

```
set $oldargs
```

Understanding getopts

Command-line parameters passed along with commands are also called **positional parameters**. Many times, we need to pass options such as −f and −v along with a positional parameter.

Let's look at an example for passing the −x or−y options along with commands.

Write shell script `getopt.sh`, as follows:

```
#!/bin/bash

USAGE="usage: $0 -x -y"

while getopts :xy: opt_char
do
  case $opt_char in
  x)
    echo "Option x was called."
    ;;
  y)
    echo "Option y was called. Argument called is $OPTARG"
    ;;
  ?)
    echo "$OPTARG is not a valid option."
    echo "$USAGE"
    ;;
  esac
done
```

Execute this program:

```
$ ./getopt.sh
```

You will learn about the switch and case statements in the next chapters. In this script, if option -x is passed, a case statement for x will be executed. If the -y option is passed, then a case statement for -y will be executed. If no option is passed, there will not be any output on the screen.

Let us run script with different options::

```
$ ./getopt.sh -x
```

The output is as follows:

```
Option y was called. Argument called is my_file.
$ ./getopt.sh -x -y my_file
Output:
Option x was called.
Option y was called. Argument called is my_file.
$ ./getopt.sh -y my_file -x
Output:
Option y was called. Argument called is my_file.
Option x was called.
```

Understanding default parameters

Many times, we may pass certain parameters from the command line, but, sometimes, we may not pass any parameters at all. We may need to initialize certain default values to certain variables.

We will review this concept through the following script.

Create script `default_argument_1.sh`, as follows:

```
#!/bin/bash
MY_PARAM=${1:-default}
echo $MY_PARAM
```

Execute the script and check the output:

```
$ chmod +x default_argument_1.sh One$ ./default_argument_1.sh OneOne$
./default_argument_1.shdefault
```

Create another `default_argument_2.sh` script:

```
#!/bin/bash
variable1=$1
variable2=${2:-$variable1}
echo $variable1
echo $variable2
```

The output is as follows:

```
[student@localhost work]$ ./default_argument_2.sh one two
one
two
[student@localhost work]$
[student@localhost work]$ ./default_argument_2.sh one
one
one
[student@localhost work]$
```

We executed the script two times:

1. When we passed two arguments, then `variable1` was `$1` and `variable2` was `$2`.

2. In the second case, when we passed only one argument, then `$1` was taken as the default argument for `$2`. Therefore, `variable1` was used as the default for `variable2`. If we do not give a second parameter, then the first parameter is taken as the default for the second parameter.

Working with arrays

An array is a list of variables. For example, we can create an array called FRUIT, which will contain the names of many fruits. The array does not have a limit on how many variables it may contain. It can contain any type of data. The first element in an array will have the index value of 0:

```
[student@localhost ~]$ FRUITS=(Mango Banana Apple)
[student@localhost ~]$ echo ${FRUITS[*]}
Mango Banana Apple
[student@localhost ~]$ echo $FRUITS[*]
Mango[*]
[student@localhost ~]$ echo ${FRUITS[2]}
Apple
[student@localhost ~]$ FRUITS[3]=Orange
[student@localhost ~]$ echo ${FRUITS[*]}
Mango Banana Apple Orange
```

Creating an array and initializing it

You will now learn about creating an array in the Bash shell.

If the array name is FRUIT, then we can create an array, as follows:

```
FRUIT[index]=value
```

Index is the integer value. It should be 0 or any positive integer value.

We can also create an array, as follows:

```
$ declare -a array_name$ declare -a arrayname=(value1 value2 value3)
```

This is an example:

```
$ declare -a fruit=('Mango' 'Banana' 'Apple' 'Orange' 'Papaya')
$ declare -a array_name=(word1 word2 word3 ...)
$ declare -a fruit=( Pears Apple Mango Banana Papaya )
$ echo ${fruit[0]}
Pears
$ echo ${fruit[1]}
Apple
$ echo "All the fruits are ${fruit[*]}"
    All the fruits are Pears Apple Mango Banana Papaya
$ echo "The number of elements in the array are ${#fruit[*]}"
    The number of elements in the array are 5
```

```
$ unset fruit
or
$ unset ${fruit[*]}
```

Accessing array values

Once we have initialized an array, we can access it, as follows:

```
${array_name[index]}
```

Create script `array_01.sh`, as follows:

```
#!/bin/bash

FRUIT[0]="Pear"
FRUIT[1]="Apple"
FRUIT[2]="Mango"
FRUIT[3]="Banana"
FRUIT[4]="Papaya"
echo "First Index: ${FRUIT[0]}"
echo "Second Index: ${FRUIT[1]}"
```

The output is as follows:

```
$ chmod +x array_01.sh$./array_01.shFirst Index: PearSecond Index: Apple
```

To display all the items from the array, use the following commands:

```
${FRUIT[*]}${FRUIT[@]}
```

Create script `array_02.sh`, as follows:

```
#!/bin/bash
FRUIT[0]="Pear"
FRUIT[1]="Apple"
FRUIT[2]="Mango"
FRUIT[3]="Banana"
FRUIT[4]="Papaya"
echo "Method One : ${FRUIT[*]}"
echo "Method Two : ${FRUIT[@]}"
```

The output is as follows:

```
$ chmod +x array_02.sh$./ array_02.shMethod One : Pear Apple Mango Banana
PapayaMethod Two : Pear Apple Mango Banana Papaya
```

Let's see a few more examples:

```
$ city[4]=Tokyo
```

The fourth member of the array, `city`, is assigned the value `Tokyo`. Since it is the only element in the array, the array size will be 1.

```
$ echo ${city[*]}Tokyo
```

The size of the array city is 1, since any other member of the array is not yet initialized.

`${city[*]}` will display the only element of the array city:

```
$ echo ${city[0]}
```

`city[0]` has no value, and neither does `city[1]` and `city[2]`.

```
$ echo ${city[4]}Tokyo
```

`city[4]` has the city name of `Tokyo`.

Assign the array countries, as follows:

```
$ countries=(USA   [3]=UK   [2]=Spain)
```

The array countries are assigned `USA` at index 0, `UK` at index 3, and `Spain` at index 2. We can observe here that it does not matter in which sequence we initialize the members of the array. They need not be given in a particular sequence.

The first element of the `countries` array is printed using the following:

```
$ echo ${countries[*]}
USA Spain UK
$ echo ${countries[0]}
USA
```

Identify the country at `index 1.`, as follows:

```
$ echo ${countries[1]}$ echo ${countries[*]}
USA Spain UK
$ echo ${countries[0]}
USA
```

Identify the country at `index 1.`, as follows:

```
$ echo ${countries[1]}
```

There is nothing stored in `countries [1].`

Use the following to identify the country at index 2:

```
$ echo ${countries[2]}Spain
```

The third element of the `countries` array, `countries [2]`, was assigned as `Spain`.

Use the following to identify the country at index 3:

```
$ echo ${countries[3]}
UK
```

The fourth element of the `countries` array, `countries [3]`, was assigned as `UK`.

Summary

In this chapter, you have learned about variables and environment variables. You have also learned about how to export environment variables, set, shift, read-only variables, command-line arguments, and about creating and handling arrays.

In the next chapter, you will learn about debugging, the `here` operator, interactive Shell scripts for taking input from a keyboard, and file handling.

Neat Tricks with Shell Scripting

6

In the last chapter, you learned about shell and environment variables. You also learned how to export environment variables, read-only variables, command-line arguments, and create/handle arrays.

In this chapter, we will cover the following topics:

- Interactive shell scripts and reading from the keyboard
- Using the here operator (<<) and here string (<<<)
- File handling
- Enabling debugging
- Syntax checking
- Shell tracing

Interactive shell scripts – reading user input

The read command is a built-in shell command for reading data from a file or keyboard.

The read command receives the input from the keyboard or a file until it receives a newline character. Then, it converts the newline character into a null character:

1. Read a value and store it in the variable, shown as follows:

```
read variable
echo $variable
```

This will receive text from the keyboard. The received text will be stored in the variable.

2. Whenever we need to display the prompt with certain text, we use the −p option. The option −p displays the text that is placed after −p on the screen:

```
#!/bin/bash
# following line will print "Enter value: " and then read data
# The received text will be stored in variable value
read -p "Enter value :  " value
```

This is the output:

```
Enter value : abcd
```

3. If the variable name is not supplied next to the read command, then the received data or text will be stored in a special built-in variable called REPLY. Let's write a simple read_01.sh script, shown as follows:

```
#!/bin/bash
echo "Where do you stay ?"
read                          # we have not supplied any option or variable
echo "You stay in $REPLY"
```

Save the file, give the permission to execute, and run the script as follows:

```
$ chmod u+x read_01.sh
$
```

This is the output:

```
"Where do you stay?"
Mumbai
"You stay at Mumbai"
```

4. We will write the script read_02.sh. This script prompts the user to enter their first and last name to greet the user with their full name:

```
#!/bin/bash
echo "Enter first Name"
read FIRSTNAME
echo "Enter Last Name"
read LASTNAME
NAME="$FIRSTNAME $LASTNAME"
echo "Name is $NAME"
```

5. For reading text and storing in multiple variables, the syntax is as follows:

```
$ read value1 value2 value3
```

Let's write the shell script, read_03.sh, shown as follows:

```
#!/bin/bash
echo "What is your name?"
read fname mname lname
echo "Your first name is : $fname"
echo "Your middle name is : $mname"
echo "Your last name is : $lname"
```

Save the file, give the permission to execute, and run the script as follows:

```
What is your name?
Ganesh Sanjiv Naik
"Your first name is : Ganesh"
"Your middle name is : Sanjiv"
"Your last name is : Naik"
```

6. Let's learn about reading a list of words and storing them in an array:

```
#!/bin/bash
echo -n "Name few cities? "
read -a cities
echo "Name of city is ${cities[2]}."
```

Save the file, give the permission to execute, and run the script as follows:

```
Name few cities? Delhi London Washington Tokyo
Name of city is Washington.
```

In this case, the list of cities is stored in the array of cities. The elements in the array are here:

```
cities[0] = Delhi
cities[1] = London
cities[2] = Washington
cities[3] = Tokyo
```

The index of the array starts with 0, and, in this case, it ends at 3. In this case, four elements are added to the cities[] array.

7. If we want the user to press the *Enter* key, then we can use the `read` command along with one unused variable, shown as follows:

```
Echo "Please press enter to proceed further "
read temp
echo "Now backup operation will be started ! "
```

Summarizing the read command with options

The following table summarizes various read command-related options that you learned in the previous sections:

Format	Meaning
read	This command will read text from a keyboard and store the received text in a built-in variable REPLY.
read value	This reads text from a keyboard or standard input and stores it into the variable value.
read first last	This will read the first word in a variable first and the remaining text of the line in a variable last. The first word is separated by white space from the remaining words in the line.
read -e	This is used in interactive shells for command-line editing. If vi editor is used, then vi commands can be used.
read -a array_name	This will store a list of words received in an array.
read -r line	Text with a backslash can be received here.
read -p prompt	This will print the prompt and wait for the user input. The received text will be stored in the variable REPLY.

The here document and the << operator

This is a special type of block of text or code. It is also a <indexentry content="<special form of I/O redirection. It can be used to feed the command list to an interactive program.

The syntax of the usage of the `here` document or the << operator is as follows:

```
command << HERE
text1 .....
text 2....
HERE
```

This tells the shell that the command should receive the data from a current source, such as the `here` document, until the pattern is received. In this case, the pattern is HERE. We have used the delimiter, HERE. We can use any other word as the delimiter, such as quit or finish. All the text reads up to the pattern, or the HERE text is used as an input for a command. The text or file received by the command is called the `Here` document:

```
$ cat << QUIT
> first input line
> ...
> last input line
> QUIT
```

The block of text inserted after and before QUIT will be treated as a file. This content will be given as input to the `cat` command. We will also see more examples with various other commands, such as `sort`, `wc`, and similar.

Let's write the script `here_01.sh`:

```
#!/bin/bash
cat << quit
  Command is $0
  First Argument is $1
  Second Argument is $2
quit
```

Save the file, give execute permissions, and run the script as follows:

```
$ chmod here_01.sh
$ ./here_01.sh Monday Tuesday
```

This will be output:

```
Command is here_01.sh
  First Argument is Monday
  Second Argument is Tuesday
```

The text block created in the preceding script between the quit words is called the here document. We can treat this here document as a separate document. It can also be treated as multiple line input redirected to a Shell script.

Let's learn a few more sample programs.

The here operator with the sort command

Let's write a script for using the sort command along with the here document:

1. Write the script here_02.sh as follows:

```
#!/bin/bash
sort << EOF
cherry
mango
apple
banana
EOF
```

2. Save the file, give the permission to execute, and run the script as follows:

```
$ chmod u+x here_02.sh
$ ./here_02.sh
```

3. The output is here:

```
apple
banana
cherry
mango
```

In this script, the here document is enclosed between the EOF pattern. We have used the here document to supply text to the sort command.

The here operator with the wc command

Let's write a script for using the wc command along with the here document:

1. Create a Shell script, here_03.sh:

```
#!/bin/bash
wc -w << EOF
There was major earthquake
```

```
On April 25, 2015
in Nepal.
There was huge loss of human life in this tragic event.
EOF
```

2. Save the file, give the permission to execute, and run the script as follows:

```
$ chmod u+x here_03.sh
$ ./here_03.sh
```

3. The output is here:

```
21
```

In this script, we have used the here document as an input for the wc command to calculate the number of words:

Tape backup using << here operator

Let's write a script for taking the tape backup by using the tar command and the here document:

1. Let's write the script here_04.sh:

```
#!/bin/bash
# We have used tar utility for archiving home folder on tape
tar -cvf /dev/st0 /home/student 2>/dev/null

# store status of tar operation in variable status
[ $? -eq 0 ] && status="Success" || status="Failed"

# Send email to administrator
mail -s 'Backup status' ganesh@levanatech.com << End_Of_Message
The backup job finished.
End date: $(date)
Status : $status
End_Of_Message
```

2. Save the file, give the permission to execute, and run the script as follows:

```
$ chmod u+x here_04.sh
$ ./here_04.sh
```

This script uses the tar command to archive the home folder in the tape device, and then it sends mail to an administrator using the mail command. We have used the here document to feed data into the mail command.

The utility ed and here operator

The ed utility is a basic type of editor. We can edit text files using this editor:

1. Write the script `here_05.sh`:

```
#!/bin/bash
# flowers.txt contains the name of flowers
cat flowers.txt
ed flowers.txt << quit
,s/Rose/Lily/g
w
q
quit
cat flowers.txt
```

2. Save the file, give the permission to execute, and run the script as follows:

```
$ chmod u+x here_05.sh
$ ./here_05.sh
```

3. The output is here:

```
Aster, Daffodil, Daisy, Jasmin, Lavender, Rose, Sunflower
59
59
Aster, Daffodil, Daisy, Jasmin, Lavender, Lily, Sunflower
```

In this script, we have passed the here document to a utility for editing the flowers.txt file. We replaced the word Rose with Lily.

A script for sending messages to all logged-in users

All users who are logged in will receive the message using the wall command:

1. Write the script `here_06.sh`:

```
#!/bin/bash
# wall utility is used for sending message to all logged in users
wall << End_Of_Message
Tomorrow, on Friday evening, we will be celebrating
Birthday of few of our colleagues.
All are requested to be present in cafeteria by 3.30 PM.
    John
End_Of_Message
echo "Message sent"
```

2. Save the file, give the permission to execute, and run the script as follows:

```
$ chmod u+x here_06.sh
$ ./here_06.sh
```

The `wall` command is used to send messages to the logged-in users. All users that are logged in will receive the message.

Using the << here operator for FTP usage and data transfer

FTP is a commonly used <indexentry content="here document:<protocol to transfer data on websites. **FTP** stands for **File Transfer Protocol**. The following steps show the <indexentry content="here document:<usage of FTP and data transfer:

1. Write the `here_07.sh` script:

```
#!/bin/bash
# Checking number of arguments passed along with command
if [ $# -lt 2 ]
then
  echo "Error, usage is:"
  echo "ftpget hostname filename [directory]."
  exit -1
fi
hostname=$1
filename=$2
directory="."          # Default value
if [ $# -ge 3 ]
then
  directory=$3
fi
ftp << End_Of_Session
open $hostname
cd $directory
get $filename
quit
End_Of_Session
echo "FTP session ended."
```

2. Save the file, give the permission to execute, and run the script as follows:

```
$ chmod u+x here_07.sh
$ ./here_07.sh ftp.somehost.com index.html WWW
```

For a successful execution of the script, we need to set up an autologin for the `ftp` command. The `here` operator does not work well when the `ftp` command asks for a username and password.

Turning off variable substitution

Enter the following script to see how to avoid a variable substitution in these files:

1. Save the script under the name `here_no.sh`, shown as follows:

```
filename="test1"
cat <<'Quoted_End_Marker'
When we add quotes before and after here
Document marker, we can include variables
Such as $USER, $PATH, $name and similar
Quoted_End_Marker
```

2. When you run this script, you will see output like the following:

```
$ bash here_no.sh
```

3. Here is the output:

```
When we add quotes before and after here
Document marker, we can include variables
Such as $USER, $PATH, $name and similar
```

This script uses an ordinary `here` file, but it turns off the variable substitution. Otherwise, you would see the values of `$HOME`, `$filename`, and `$USER` in the output instead of the literal text. All of this is done by magically enclosing the end marker, `Quoted_End_Marker`, in quotes at the original reference. Do not enclose the marker in quotes at the end of the `here` file.

The here string and the <<< operator

The `here` string is used for input redirection from <indexentry content="<<text or a variable. Input is mentioned on the same line within single quotes (`' '`).

The syntax is as follows:

```
$ command <<< 'string'
```

1. Let's see the following example, hereString_01.sh:

```
#!/bin/bash
wc -w <<< 'Good Morning and have a nice day !'
```

2. Save the file, give the permission, and run the script as follows:

```
$ chmod u+x hereString_01.sh
$ ./hereString_01.sh
```

3. Here is the output:

```
8
```

In this example, the string Good Morning and have a nice day ! is called as the here string.

File handling

In this section, you will learn about handling files for reading and writing. In Chapter 8, *Automating Decision-Making in Scripts*, you will learn about checking various attributes of files along with decision-making constructs, such as if, case, and similar.

Introducing file handling

The exec command is very interesting. Whenever we run any command in a shell, a new subshell or process gets created, and the command runs in this newly created process. When we run any command as an argument to the exec command, exec will replace the current shell with the command to be executed. It does not create or spawn a new process to run the command.

Using exec to assign a file descriptor (fd) to file

In the Bash shell environment, every process has three files opened by default. These are standard input, display, and error. The file descriptors associated with them are 0, 1, and 2 respectively. In the Bash shell, we can assign the file descriptor to any input or output file. These are called file descriptors.

The syntax for declaring `output.txt` as output is as follows:

```
exec fd > output.txt
```

This command will declare the number `fd` as an output file descriptor.

The syntax for closing the file is as follows:

```
exec fd<&-
```

To close `fd`, which is 5, enter the following:

```
exec 5<&-
```

We will try to understand these concepts by writing scripts.

Understanding the opening, writing, and closing of a file

Let's understand the opening, closing, and writing of a file.

Write a Shell script `file_01.sh`, shown as follows:

```
#!/bin/bash
# We will open file for writing purpose
# We are assigning descriptor number 3 for file sample_out.txt
exec 3> sample_out.txt

# We are sending output of command "echo" to sample_out.txt file
echo "This is a test message for sample_out.txt file" >&3

# Run command date & store output in file sample_out.txt
date >&3

# Closing file with file descriptor 3
exec 3<&-
```

Save the file, give the permission to execute, and run the script as follows:

```
$ chmod u+x file_01.sh
$ ./file_01.sh
$ cat sample_out.txt
```

This should produce the following output:

```
This is a test message for sample_out.txt file
Tue Sep 29 23:19:22 IST 2015
```

Understanding reading from a file

Let's write a script to read from a file:

Write the script `file_02.sh`, shown as follows:

```
#!/bin/bash
# We will open file sample_input.txt for reading purpose.
# We are assigning descriptor 3 to the file.
exec 3< sample_input.txt

cat <&3
# Closing file
exec 3<&-
```

Save the file, give the permission to execute, and run the script as follows:

```
$ chmod u+x file_02..sh
```

We will create the `sample_input.txt` file as follows:

```
$ echo "Hello to All" > sample_input.txt
```

Run the script and check the result:

```
$ ./file_02.sh
```

This should produce the following output:

```
Hello to All
```

Understanding reading and writing to a file

In the earlier examples, we opened the file either for reading or writing. Now we will see how to open the file for reading and writing purposes:

```
exec fd<> fileName
```

If the file descriptor number is not specified, then 0 will be used in its place. The file will be created if it does not exist. This procedure is useful for updating files.

Let's understand the following script.

Write the shell script `file_03.sh` as follows:

```bash
#!/bin/bash
file_name="sample_out.txt"
# We are assing fd number 3 to file.
# We will be doing read and write operations on file
exec 3<> $file_name

# Writing to file
echo """
 Do not dwell in the past,
 do not dream of the future,
 concentrate the mind on the present moment. - Buddha
""" >&3
# closing file with fd number 3
exec 3>&-
```

Using the read command on a file descriptor (fd)

We can use the `read` command to get data from a file to store it in variables.
The procedure for using the `read` command to get a text from a file is as follows:

```
read -u fd variable1 variable2 ... variableN
```

Reading from one file and writing to another file

Now we will see how to read from one file and write to another. Let's write the
`file_04.sh` script as follows:

```bash
#!/bin/bash
# We are assigning descriptor 3 to in_file.txt
exec 3< in_file.txt
# We are assigning descriptor 4 to out_file.txt
exec 4> out_file.txt

# We are reading first line of input.txt
read -u 3 line

echo $line

echo "Writing content of in_file.txt to out_file.txt"
echo  "Line 1 - $line " >&4
```

```
# Closing both the files
exec 3<&-
exec 4<&-
```

Save the file, give the permission to execute, and run the script as follows:

```
$ chmod u+x file_04.sh
$ echo "Sun is at the centre of Solar System." > in_file.txt
$ cat in_file.txt
```

This should produce the following outputs:

```
Sun is at the centre of Solar System.
$ ./file_04.sh

Sun is at the centre of Solar System.
Writing content of in_file.txt to out_file.txt
$ cat out_file.txt

Line 1 - Sun is at the center of Solar System.
```

In this example, we read the complete line in the variable line and we use the same variable to write it to another file.

Let's write one more script, file_05.sh, to get the hostname and addresses:

```
#!/bin/sh

cd /etc/hosts hosts2

grep -v '^#' hosts2 > hosts3

exec 3< hosts3      # opening hosts3 as input file

exec 4> hostsfinal  # opening hostsfinal as output file

read <& 3 address1 name_1 extra_info
read <& 3 address2 name_2 extra_info

echo $name_1 $address1 >& 4
echo $name_2 $address2 >& 4

exec 3<&-      # Closing hosts3
exec 4<&-      # Closing hostsfinal
```

In this script, we used the variables address1, name_1, extra_info, address2, and name_2 to store useful information.

Displaying the file descriptor information from the /proc folder

We will write the script to display the actual file descriptors associated with the file.

Let's write the `file_06.sh` script, shown as follows:

```bash
#!/bin/bash
# we are assigning file descriptor 3 to input file test.txt
exec 3< test.txt
# we are assigning file descriptor 4 to output.txt
exec 4> output.txt
# we are using read command to read line from file
read -u 3 line
echo "Process id of current process is $$"
my_pid=$$
echo "Currently following files are opened by $0 script :"
ls -l /proc/$my_pid/fd

# We are closing both files test.txt and output.txt
exec 3<&-
exec 4>&-
```

File handling - reading line by line

You will learn how to use the `while` loop and the `read` command to read a file line by line. You will learn more about the `while` loop in the upcoming chapters.

Let's write the `file_07.sh` script, as follows:

```bash
#!/bin/bash
echo "Enter the name of file for reading"
read file_name
exec<$file_name
while read var_line
do
  echo $var_line
done
```

For executing the preceding script, we will need to create a file with some text in it. Then, we can pass this filename for reading purposes.

Executing the command and storing the results in a file

The following is the syntax for storing the output of a command in a file:

```
Command >& fd
./script >& fd
```

The following is the illustrative example script, `file_08.sh`:

```
#!/bin/bash
exec 4> output.txt
cat /proc/cpuinfo  >&4
exec 3<&-
```

Save the file, give the permission to execute, and run the script as follows:

```
$ chmod u+x file_08.sh
$ ./file_08.sh
```

Here's the output:

```
[student@localhost work]$ ./file_08.sh
[student@localhost work]$ cat output.txt
processor       : 0
vendor_id       : GenuineIntel
cpu family      : 6
model           : 158
model name      : Intel(R) Core(TM) i5-7400 CPU @ 3.00GHz
stepping        : 9
microcode       : 0x5e
cpu MHz         : 2999.525
cache size      : 6144 KB
physical id     : 0
siblings        : 1
core id         : 0
cpu cores       : 1
apicid          : 0
initial apicid  : 0
fpu             : yes
```

In this example, we have executed the command `cat /proc/cpuinfo` and we have stored the output in the file, `output.txt`.

Summarizing usage of the exec command

The following is a summary of the exec command for using various file handling-related operations:

Command	What it does
`exec` command	This command will replace shell and execute it. Therefore, it will not return to its original shell, which started it.
`exec > data.txt`	This opens `data.txt` for writing standard output.
`exec < data.txt`	This opens `data.txt` for reading standard input.
`exec 3< data.txt`	This opens `data.txt` for reading with descriptor 3.
`sort <&3`	This will sort the `data.txt` file.
`exec 4> data.txt`	This opens `data.txt` for writing with descriptor 4.
`ll >&4`	The output of `ll` is redirected to `data.txt`.
`exec 6<&5`	This makes `fd 6` a copy of `fd 5`.
`exec 4<&-`	This closes `fd 4`.

Debugging

In the very old days of computer technology, the initial problems with computers were due to real insects. Due to this, fault finding was later called finding the bug. Therefore, the process of finding and fixing the problems in computers was called debugging.

The process of debugging involves the following:

- Finding out what has gone wrong
- Fixing the problem

In the actual debugging process, you need to do the following:

- Understand the error message and find out what the problem is with the script.
- Find the error location in the script.

- Locate the line number from the error message. The following are a few error messages:

  - `debug_sp: line 11: [7: command not found]`
  - `file: line 6: unexpected EOF while looking for matching `"'`

    These messages inform the user about the line numbers of the script that contain errors.

- Correct the issue or problematic part of code. We may have to read the line as well as look backward from this line number for any possible reason for the error.

Debugging mode – disabling the shell (option -n)

In the Bash shell, the `-n` option is a shortcut for `noexec` (as in no execution). This option tells the shell not to run the commands. Instead, the shell just checks for syntax errors.

We can test the script as follows:

```
$ bash -n hello.sh
```

The `-n` option will tell the Bash shell to check the syntax in the Shell script but not to execute the Shell script.

Another way to do this is as follows:

```
#!/bin/bash  -n
We have modified shebang line.
```

In this case, we can test the Shell script as follows:

```
$ chmod u+x hello.sh
$ ./hello.sh
```

This option is safe, since the shell commands are not executed. We can catch incomplete if, for, while, case, and similar programming constructs as well as many more syntactical errors.

Let's write `debug_01.sh`:

```
#!/bin/bash
echo -n "Commands in bin directory are : $var"

for var in $(ls )
do
        echo -n -e "$var     "
do
# no error if "done" is typed instead of "do"
```

Save the file, give the permission to execute, and run the script as follows:

```
$ chmod  u+x debug_01.sh
$ ./debug_01.sh
```

This should produce the following output:

```
Commands in bin directory are : ./hello.sh: line 7: syntax error near
unexpected token `do'
./hello.sh: line 7: `do'
$ bash -n debug_01.sh
```

This should produce the following output:

```
hello.sh: line 7: syntax error near unexpected token `do'
hello.sh: line 7: `do'
```

Debugging mode - displaying commands (option -v)

The -v option tells the shell to run in **verbose** mode. In practice, this means that the shell will echo each command prior to executing the command. This will be useful in locating the line of script that has created an error.

We can enable the script execution with the -v option as follows:

```
$ bash -v hello.sh
```

Another way is by modifying the shebang line as follows:

```
#!/bin/bash  -v
```

In this case, we can run the script with the −v option as follows:

```
$ chmod u+x hello.sh
$ ./hello.sh
```

Let's write the debug_02.sh script as follows:

```
#!/bin/bash
echo "Hello $LOGNAME"
echo "Today is `date`
echo "Your present working directory is $PWD
echo Good-bye $LOGNAME
```

Save the file, give the permission to execute, and run the script as follows:

```
$ chmod u+x debug_02.sh
$ ./debug_02.sh
```

This should produce the following output:

```
Hello student
Today is Fri May 1 00:18:52 IST 2015
Your present working directory is /home/student/work
Good-bye student
```

Let's enable the −v option for debugging, and run the script again as follows:

```
$ bash −v debug_02.sh
```

This should produce the following output:

```
#!/bin/bash
echo "Hello $LOGNAME"
"Hello student"
echo "Today is `date`
date
"Today is Fri May 1 00:18:52 IST 2015
echo "Your present working directory is $PWD
"Your present working directory is /home/student/work
echo Good-bye $LOGNAME
Good-bye student
```

Debugging mode – the tracing execution (option -x)

The -x option, short for xtrace or execution trace, tells the shell to echo each command after performing the substitution steps. Thus, we will see the value of variables and commands.

We can trace the execution of the Shell script as follows:

```
$ bash -x hello.sh
```

Instead of the previous way, we can modify the shebang line as follows:

```
#!/bin/bash   -x
```

Let's test the earlier debug_01.sh script as follows:

```
$ bash -x hello.sh
```

Output:

```
$ bash -x debug_02.sh
+ echo Hello student
Hello student
+ date
+ echo The date is Fri May 1 00:18:52 IST 2015
The date is Fri May 1 00:18:52 IST 2015
+ echo Your home shell is /bin/bash
Your home shell is /bin/bash
+ echo Good-bye student
Good-bye student
```

Let's try the following programs with the -n, -v, -f, and -x options. Here's a sample program,-debug_03.sh:

```
#!/bin/bash
echo "Total number of parameters are = $#"
echo "Script name = $0"
echo "First Parameter is $1"
echo "Second Parameter is $2"
echo "All parameters are = $*"
echo "File names starting with f* in current folder are :"
ls f*
```

Save the file, give the permission to execute, and run the script as follows:

```
$ chmod u+x debug_03.sh
$ ./debug_03.sh One Two
```

This should produce the following output:

```
"Total number of parameters are = 2"
"Script name = ./debug_03.sh"
"First Parameter is India"
"Second Parameter is Delhi"
"All parameters are = India Delhi"
"File names starting with debug_02.sh debug_03.sh in current folder
are: "
debug_02.sh   debug_03.sh
```

Let's test the same script with the −n option, which will check for syntax errors:

```
$ bash -n debug_03.sh One Two
```

Let's test the same script with the −v option:

```
$ bash -v debug_03.sh One Two
```

This should produce the following output:

```
#!/bin/bash
echo "Total number of parameters are = $#"
"Total number of parameters are = 2"
echo "Script name = $0"
"Script name = debug_03.sh"
echo "First Parameter is $1"
"First Parameter is India"
echo "Second Parameter is $2"
"Second Parameter is Delhi"
echo "All parameters are = $*"
"All parameters are = India Delhi"
echo "File names starting with d* in current folder are :"
"File names starting with debug_02.sh debug_03.sh in current folder
are: "
ls d*
debug_02.sh   debug_03.sh
```

Let us test the same script with the −x option:

```
$ bash -x debug_03.sh One Two
```

This should produce the following output:

```
+ echo $'342200234Total' number of parameters are = $'2342200235'
"Total number of parameters are = 2"
+ echo $'342200234Script' name = $'debug_03.sh342200235'
"Script name = debug_03.sh"
+ echo $'342200234First' Parameter is $'India342200235'
"First Parameter is India"
+ echo $'342200234Second' Parameter is $'Delhi342200235'
"Second Parameter is Delhi"
+ echo $'342200234All' parameters are = India $'Delhi342200235'
"All parameters are = India Delhi"
+ echo $'342200234File' names starting with debug_02.sh debug_03.sh in
current folder are $':342200234'
"File names starting with debug_02.sh debug_03.sh in current folder
are: "
+ ls debug_02.sh debug_03.sh
debug_02.sh   debug_03.sh
```

Let's test one more program, which will give a syntax error during the −n and −x options debugging. Write the debug_04.sh Shell script as follows:

```
#!/bin/bash
echo "Commands in bin directory are : $var"

for var in $(ls )
do
        echo −n −e "$var     "
do
```

Save the file, give the permission to execute, and run the script as follows:

```
$ chmod u+x debug_04.sh
$ bash −n debug_04.sh
```

This should produce the following output:

```
debug_04.sh: line 7: syntax error near unexpected token `do'
debug_04.sh: line 7: `do'
```

The preceding program has a syntax error on line number 7. The word do has an error. We need to change word do to done.

Summarizing the debugging options for the Bash shell

The following is a summary of various debugging options used for debugging, such as −x, −v, and −n with their details:

```
$ bash -n script_name   // interpretation without execution
$ bash -v script_name   // Display commands in script
$ bash -x script_name   // Trace the execution of script
$ bash -xv script_name   // Enable options x and v for debugging
$ bash +xv script_name   //Disable options x and v for debugging
```

Using the set command

Most of the time, we invoke the debugging mode from the first line of script. This debugging mode will remain active until the last line of code. But many times, we may need to enable debugging for a particular section of script. By using the set command, we can enable and disable debugging at any point in our shell script:

```
set -x
section of script
set +x
```

Consider the following script:

```
#!/bin/bash

str1="USA"
str2="Canada";

[ $str1 = $str2 ]
echo $?

Set -x

[ $str1 != $str2 ]
echo $?

[ -z $str1 ]
echo $?

Set +x

[ -n $str2 ]
```

```
echo $?

Exit 0
```

In this case, the debugging will be enabled after the set −x and will be disabled immediately after the set +x.

Summary of debugging options for the set command

The following table summarizes the various options for the set command:

Short notation	Result
set −f	Disables globing. In this case, the filename expansions using wildcards or meta-characters will be disabled.
set −v	This will print the shell script lines as they are read by the shell.
set −x	This option will display each line after the variable substitution and command expansion, but before execution by the shell. This option is often called shell tracing.
set −n	This reads all commands and checks the syntax, but does not execute them.

The vi editor setting for debugging

For general debugging, we can use the vi editor along with certain options.

During debugging, many times we search for a pattern throughout the complete document. It is preferable to highlight the searched item. We will enable search pattern highlighting by using the following command in the vi editor when the document is opened:

```
:set hlsearch
:set ic
```

We can even modify the vi editor configuration file-.exrc or .vimrc so that we need not give the previous command again and again.

Good practices for Shell scripts

If we follow certain good practices, then we will face errors. Even if errors are found, these will be easier to debug:

1. Clear and tidy the script.
2. Try to properly indent the programming constructs, such as if, for, while, and other similar loops:

```
if [ $rate -lt 3 ]
then
  echo "Sales tax rate is too small."
fi
```

3. Do not put multiple commands on the same line by using ;.
4. Use descriptive variable names, such as *salary*, instead of *sa*. In very complex Shell scripts, non-descriptive variable names will make debugging very difficult.
5. Store the file and directory names in variables instead of typing them again and again. If any change is required in the directory path, then making the change in the variable at one place will be sufficient:

```
WORKING_DIR=$HOME/work
if [ -e $WORKING_DIR]
then
  # Do something....
fi
```

6. Use comments for an easier understanding of the script. This will make debugging easier to others. If it contains tricky or complex commands, then, even after a few months, we will need comments to understand our own script. A cute little trick today may become a challenge tomorrow.
7. Print informative error messages. Write simpler scripts. Use simpler if, case, for, and or functions. It has been practically observed that if scripts are simpler, then such scripts are easy to maintain over a long period of time, such as a few years.
8. Test the script again and again with various test scenarios and test cases. Check for all possibilities of human error, such as bad input, insufficient arguments, non-existent files, and similar possibilities.

Summary

In this chapter, you learned about debugging, the here operator, interactive shell scripts for taking input from the keyboard, and file handling.

In the next chapter, you will learn about arithmetic and various operations, such as addition, subtraction, multiplication, division, and the extraction of the modulus of numerical variables.

7
Performing Arithmetic Operations in Shell Scripts

In the last chapter, you learned about debugging, the `here` operator, interactive shell scripts for taking input from the keyboard, and file handling.

In this chapter, we will cover the following arithmetic operations topics:

- Addition
- Subtraction
- Multiplication
- Division
- Modulus

We can perform arithmetic operations in various ways, such as using `declare`, `let`, `expr`, and arithmetic expressions. You will also learn about representing numbers in different bases, such as binary, octal, and hex.

Using a declare command for arithmetic

Whenever we declare any variable, by default, this variable stores the string type of data. We cannot do arithmetic operations on them. We can declare a variable as an integer by using the `declare` command. Such variables are declared as integers; if we try to assign a string to them, then bash assigns 0 to these variables.

Bash will report an error if we try to assign fractional values (floating points) to integer variables.

We can create an integer variable called `value`, shown as follows:

```
$ declare -i value
```

We tell the shell that the variable value is of type integer. Otherwise, the shell treats all variables as character strings:

- If we try to assign the `name` string to the integer variable `value`, then the `value` variable will be assigned the 0 value by the Bash shell:

```
$ value=name
$ echo $value
0
```

- We need to enclose numbers between double quotes, otherwise we should not use a space in arithmetic expressions:

```
$ value=4 + 4
bash: +: command not found
```

- When we remove white spaces, the error also gets removed, and the arithmetic operation takes place:

```
$ value=4+4
$ echo $value
8
```

- We can perform a multiplication operation as follows:

```
$ value=4*3
$ echo $value
12
$ value="4 * 5"
$ echo $value
20
```

- Since we have enclosed numbers in " ", the multiplication operation is performed. Due to double quotes (" "), the * operator was not used as a wildcard (*):

```
$ value=5.6
bash: 5.6: syntax error: invalid arithmetic operator (error token is
".6").
```

Since we have declared the `value` variable as an integer variable, when we initialize the variable with a floating point number, the error gets displayed by the Bash shell.

Listing integers

If we want to see all declared integer variables along with their values, then we must give the following command:

```
$ declare -i
```

This should produce the following output:

```
declare -ir BASHPID=""
declare -ir EUID="1001"
declare -i HISTCMD=""
declare -i LINENO=""
declare -i MAILCHECK="60"
declare -i OPTIND="1"
declare -ir PPID="1966"
declare -i RANDOM=""
declare -ir UID="1001"
```

Using the let command for arithmetic

We can use the bash built-in command `let` for performing arithmetic operations. To get more information about `let`, type the following:

```
$ help let
```

This should produce the following output of this command:

```
[student@localhost ~]$ help let
let: let arg [arg ...]
    Evaluate arithmetic expressions.

    Evaluate each ARG as an arithmetic expression.  Evaluation is done in
    fixed-width integers with no check for overflow, though division by 0
    is trapped and flagged as an error.  The following list of operators is
    grouped into levels of equal-precedence operators.  The levels are listed
    in order of decreasing precedence.

        id++, id--      variable post-increment, post-decrement
        ++id, --id      variable pre-increment, pre-decrement
        -, +            unary minus, plus
        !, ~            logical and bitwise negation
        **              exponentiation
        *, /, %         multiplication, division, remainder
        +, -            addition, subtraction
        <<, >>          left and right bitwise shifts
        <=, >=, <, >    comparison
        ==, !=          equality, inequality
        &               bitwise AND
        ^               bitwise XOR
        |               bitwise OR
        &&              logical AND
        ||              logical OR
        expr ? expr : expr
                        conditional operator
        =, *=, /=, %=,
        +=, -=, <<=, >>=,
```

Let's start using the `let` command:

```
$ value=6
$ let value=value+1
$ echo $value
7
$ let "value=value+4"
$ echo $value
11
$ let "value+=1"
#above expression evaluates as value=value+1
$ echo $value
12
```

A summary of operators available with the `let` command follows:

- Operation: `Operator`
- Unary minus: -
- Unary plus: +
- Logical NOT: !
- Bitwise NOT (negation): ~
- Multiply: *

- Divide: /
- Remainder: %
- Subtract: –
- Add: +

Prior to Bash 2.x, the following operators were not available:

- Bitwise left shift: <<
- Bitwise right shift: >>
- Equal to and not equal to: ==, !=
- Comparison operators: <=, >=, <, >
- Bitwise AND: &
- Bitwise OR: |
- Bitwise exclusive OR: ^
- Logical AND: &&
- Logical OR: ||
- Assignment and shortcut assignment: = *=/= %= -= += >>= <<= &= |= ^=

Using the expr command for arithmetic

We can use the `expr` command for arithmetic operations. The `expr` command is an external command; the binary of the `expr` command is stored in the folder called `/usr/bin/expr`.

Perform an addition operation as follows:

```
$ expr 40 + 2
42
```

Perform a subtraction operation as follows:

```
$ expr 42 - 2
40
```

Perform a division operation as follows:

```
$ expr 40 / 10
4
```

Perform a modulus (getting remainder) operation as follows:

```
$ expr 42 % 10
2
$ expr 4 * 10
expr: syntax error
```

With the `expr` command, we cannot use * for multiplication. We need to use *
for multiplication:

```
$ expr "4 * 10"
4 * 10
$ expr 4 * 10
40
```

We will write a simple script to add two numbers. Write the shell script,
`arithmetic_01.sh` as follows:

```
!/bin/bash
x=5
y=2
z=`expr $x + $y`
echo $z
```

Test the script as follows:

```
$ chmod +x arithmetic_01.sh
$ ./arithmetic_01.sh
```

This is the output:

```
7
```

Let's write a script to perform all the basic arithmetic operations. Write the Shell script
called `arithmetic_02.sh` as follows:

```
#!/bin/bash
var1=30
var2=20
echo `expr $var1 + $var2`          # Arithmetic Addition
echo `expr $var1 - $var2`          # Arithmetic Subtraction
echo `expr $var1 * $var2`          # Arithmetic Multiplication
echo `expr $var1 / $var2`          # Arithmetic Division
echo `expr $var1 % $var2`          # Arithmetic Modular Division
                                   # (Remainder)
```

Let us test the script:

```
$ chmod +x arithmetic_02.sh
$ ./arithmetic_02.sh
```

This is the output:

```
50
10
600
1
10
```

Using an arithmetic expansion

We can use two different ways for evaluating arithmetic expressions:

```
$(( expression ))
$[ expression ]
```

Learn arithmetic operations using the preceding mentioned arithmetic expansion:

```
$ a=10
$ b=20
$ c=$(( a + b ))
$ echo $c
```

During arithmetic operations, we may need to find the square or cube of any given number. These operations are called exponent operations. We can perform exponent operations as follows:

```
$ a=5
$ b=3
$ expo=$[ $a ** $b ]      # This is equivalent to ab
$ echo $expo
125
```

This is the result of the 5^3 operations:

Another way to do arithmetic expansions is as follows:

```
$ B=10
$ A=$[B + 10]
$ echo $A
20
$ echo $[ 3 + 4 - 5 ]
```

```
2
$ echo $[ 3 + 4 * 5]
23
```

Arithmetic multiplication has precedence over addition. Therefore, `4*5` was performed first, and the addition of `3+20` was performed later on:

```
$ echo $[(3 + 4) * 5]
35
$ echo $(( 3 + 4 ))
7
$ echo $(( 6 / 0 ))
bash: 6/0: division by 0 ( error token is "0")
```

We will use many of the preceding arithmetic techniques for doing the same addition operation and check the result.

Let's write an interactive script called `arithmetic_03.sh` as follows:

```
#!/bin/bash
echo "Enter first value"
read number_1
echo "Enter second value"
read number_2
total=`expr $number_1 + $number_2`
echo $total
sum=$(($number_1 + $number_2))
echo "sum is "$sum
echo "Sum is $[ $number_1+$number_2 ]"
```

Let us test the script:

```
$ chmod +x arithmetic_03.sh
$ ./arithmetic_03.sh
```

Output:

```
Enter first value
10
Enter second value
5
15
Sum is 15
Sum is 15
```

The preceding Shell script shows that even if we use any of the previous techniques, the result remains the same.

Let's write a shell script called `arithmetic_04.sh` as follows:

```
#!/bin/bash
# Interactive Shell Script Demonstrating Arithmetic Operators
echo "Enter First value"
read number_1
echo "Enter Second value"
read number_2
echo $(($number_1 + $number_2))
echo $(($number_1 / $number_2)) # Division of two numbers
```

Let's test the program as follows:

```
$ chmod +x arithmetic_04.sh
$ ./arithmetic_04.sh
```

This should produce the following output:

```
Enter First value
10
Enter Second value
5
15
2
```

We will write one more script with a different technique. Let's write the Shell script `arithmetic_05.sh` as follows:

```
#!/bin/bash
# Script is For Demonstrating Arithmetic
var1=10
var2=20
echo $(($var1+$var2))    # Adding Two Values
echo $(($var1-$var2))    # Subtract Two Values
echo $(($var1*$var2))    # Multiply Two Values
echo $(($var1%$var2))    # Remainder
```

Let's test the program here:

```
$ chmod +x arithmetic_05.sh
$ ./arithmetic_05.sh
```

This should produce the following output:

```
30
-10
200
10
```

We will write a script to add five numbers that are passed from a command line. Let's write the Shell script, `arithmetic_06.sh` as follows:

```
#!/bin/bash
# Write a shell script which will receive 5 numbers from command line
# and print their sum.
echo "Sum of Five Numbers is:" $(($1 + $2 + $3 + $4 + $5))
```

Let's test the program:

```
$ chmod +x arithmetic_06.sh
$ ./arithmetic_06.sh 10 20 30 40 50
```

This should produce the following output:

```
Sum of Five Numbers is: 150
```

Let's write the Shell script, `arithmetic_07.sh` as follows for finding the cube, quotient, and remainder:

```
#!/bin/bash

x=99

(( cube = x * x * x ))
(( quotient = x / 5 ))
(( remainder = x % 5 ))

echo "The cube of $x is $cube."
echo "The quotient of $x divided by 5 is $quotient."
echo "The remainder of $x divided by 5 is $remainder."

# Note the use of parenthesis to controlling arithmetic operator
# precedence evaluation.
(( y = 2 * (quotient * 5 + remainder) ))
echo "Two times $x is $y."
```

Let's test the program:

```
$ chmod +x arithmetic_07.sh
$ ./arithmetic_07.sh
```

This should produce the following output:

```
The cube of 99 is 970299.
The quotient of 99 divided by 5 is 19.
The remainder of 99 divided by 5 is 4.
Two times 99 is 198.
```

Binary, octal, and hex arithmetic operations

Integer values can be represented in decimal, binary, octal, or hex numeric notations. By default, integer values are represented in decimal notation. Binary numbers have base 2. Octal numbers use base 8. Hexadecimal numbers use base 16. We will learn about various notations with examples in this section.

This is the syntax:

variable=base#number-in-that-base

Let's understand the preceding syntax with examples:

- Decimal representation:

```
$ declare -i x=21
$ echo $x
21
```

- Binary representation:

```
$ x=2#10101
$ echo $x
21
```

- Octal representation:

```
$ declare -i x
$ x=8#25
$ echo $x
21
```

- Hexadecimal representation:

```
$ declare -i x
$ x=16#15
$ echo $x
21
```

In the preceding examples, we displayed the decimal 21 value in binary, octal, and hexadecimal representations.

Floating-point arithmetic

In the Bash shell, we can only perform integer arithmetic. If we want to perform arithmetic involving a floating point or fractional values, then we will need to use various other utilities, such as awk, bc, and similar.

Let's see an example of using the utility called bc:

```
$ echo "scale=2; 15 / 2" | bc
7.50
```

For using the bc utility, we need to configure a scale parameter. Scale is the number of significant digits to the right of the decimal point. We have told the bc utility to calculate 15 / 2, and then display the result with the scale of 2.

Another example is the following:

```
$ bc
((83.12 + 32.13) * 37.3)
4298.82
```

Many things can be done with the bc utility, such as all types of arithmetic operations including binary and unary operations; it has many defined mathematical functions. It has its own programming syntax.

You can get more information about the bc utility at: http://www.gnu.org/software/bc/.

Let's look at using awk for floating-point arithmetic:

```
$ result=`awk -v a=3.1 -v b=5.2 'BEGIN{printf "%.2fn",a*b}'`
$ echo $result
16.12
```

You will be learning more about awk programming in the coming chapters. Therefore, we will not get into a detailed discussion of awk in this session.

Let's write a few more Shell scripts using the arithmetic programming skills we have learned so far.

Let's write the Bash shell script arithmetic_08.sh to determine whether an input integer is even or odd:

```
#!/bin/bash
echo "Please enter a value"
read x
```

```
y=`expr $x % 2`
if test $y -eq 0
then
    echo "Entered number is even"
else
    echo "Entered number is odd"
fi
```

Let's test the program:

```
$ chmod +x arithmetic_08.sh
$ ./arithmetic_08.sh
Output:
"Enter a number"
5
"Number is odd"
"Enter a number"
6
"Number is even"
```

Let's write the script `arithmetic_09.sh` to find the length of an input string:

```
#!/bin/bash
echo "Please Enter the String:"
read str
len=`echo $str | wc -c`
let len=len-1
echo "length of string = $len"
```

Let's test the script:

```
$ chmod +x arithmetic_09.sh
$ ./arithmetic_09.sh
```

This should produce the following output:

```
Enter String:
Hello World
length of string = 11
```

Let's write a script to calculate the area and circumference of a rectangle and circle.

Write the shell script `arithmetic_10.sh` as follows:

```
#!/bin/bash
echo "Please enter the length, width and radius"
read length width radius
areaRectangle=`expr $length * $width `
```

```
temp=`expr $length + $width `
perimeterRect=`expr 2 * $temp`
areaCircle=`echo 3.14 * $radius * $radius | bc`
circumferenceCircle=`echo 2 * 3.14 * $radius | bc`
echo "Area of rectangle = $areaRectangle"
echo "Perimeter of Rectangle = $perimeterRect."
echo "Area of circle = $areaCircle."
echo "Circumference of circle = $circumferenceCircle"
echo
```

Let's test the program:

```
$ chmod +x arithmetic_10.sh
$ ./arithmetic_10.sh
```

This should produce the following output:

```
Enter the length, width and radius
5 10 5
Area of rectangle = 50
Perimeter of Rectangle = 30
Area of circle = 78.50
Circumference of circle = 31.40
```

Summary

In this chapter, you learned about performing arithmetic operations in various ways, such as using declare, let, expr, and arithmetic expressions. You also learned about representing numbers in different bases such as hex, octal, and binary. You learned about using the bc utility to perform floating-point or fractional arithmetic.

In the next chapter, you will learn about automatic decision-making by working with tests and using if-else, case, select, for, while, and do while. You will also learn to control loops using break and continue statements.

8
Automating Decision-Making in Scripts

In the last chapter, you learned about performing arithmetic operations in various ways, such as using `declare`, `let`, `expr`, and arithmetic expressions. You also learned about representing numbers in different bases, such as hex, octal, and binary, and using the `bc` utility for performing floating point or fractional arithmetic.

In real-world scripts, it is not just a sequential execution of commands, we need to check certain conditions or proceed according to certain logic, and then the script should continue executing. This is precisely what we do with automation. Automation refers to performing tasks, the sequence of which will change according to changes in the programming environment. A simple example would be to check whether a directory is present; if present, then change to that directory. Otherwise create a new directory and proceed. All these activities come under decision-making in shell scripts.

In this chapter, we will cover the following topics:

- Working with `test`
- Using `if-else`
- Switching `case`
- Using `select`

Checking the exit status of commands

Automation using shell scripts involves checking whether an earlier command executed successfully, whether a file is present, and so on. You will learn various constructs such as `if`, `case`, and so on, where we will need to check whether certain conditions are true or false. Accordingly, our script should conditionally execute various commands.

Let's enter the following command:

```
$ ls
```

Using the Bash shell, we can check whether the preceding command executed successfully as follows:

```
$ echo $?
```

The preceding command will return 0 if the `ls` command executed successfully. The result will be non-zero, such as 1 or 2 or any other non-zero number, if the command has failed. The Bash shell stores the status of the last command execution in a variable. If we need to check the status of the last command execution, then we should check the content of the variable.

Let's take the following example:

```
$ x=10
$ y=20
$ (( x < y ))
$ echo $?
0
```

This indicates that the `$(( x < y ))` expression has executed successfully.

Let's look at the same concept in the case of string handling:

```
$ name=Ganesh
$ grep "$name"  /etc/passwd
  Ganesh:9ZAC5G:6283:40:Ganesh Naik:/home/ganesh:/bin/sh
$ echo $?
0
```

Since the user `Ganesh` has already been created on the computer, the string `Ganesh` was found in the `/etc/passwd` file.

```
$ name=John
$ grep "$name" /etc/passwd
$ echo $?
1           # non zero values means error
```

Since the user `John` was not found in the `/etc/passwd` file, the `grep` command returned a non-zero value. In scripts, we can use this during automation.

Understanding the test command

Let's now understand the `test` command.

Using the test command

Let's look at the following example to check the content or value of expressions:

```
$ test $name=Ganesh
$ echo $?
0 if success and 1 if failure.
```

In the preceding example, we want to check whether the content of the variable name is the same as `Ganesh` and `?`. To check this, we have used the `test` command. The `test` command will store the result of the comparison in the `?` variable.

We can use the following syntax for the preceding `test` command. In this case, we used `[ ]` instead of the `test` command. We've enclosed the expression to be evaluated in square brackets:

```
$ [[ $name = Ganesh ]]       # Brackets replace the test command
$ echo $?
0
```

During the evaluation of expressions by `test`, we can even use wildcard expressions:

```
$ [[ $name = [Gg]????? ]]
$ echo $?
0
```

Therefore, we can either use the `test` command or square brackets for checking or evaluating expressions. Since word splitting will be performed on variables, if we are using text with white spaces, then we will need to enclose the text inside double quotes, " ".

Using the test command with double brackets

Let's consider a case where we want to check whether there is the name `Ganesh` and whether his friend is `John`. In this case, we will have multiple expressions to be checked using the AND operator, `&&`. In such a case, we can use the following syntax:

```
$ [[ $name == Ganesh && $friend == "John" ]]
```

Another way to do this is as follows:

```
[ $name == Ganesh ] && [ $friend == "John" ]
```

We used double brackets in the preceding expressions.

Here, we want to evaluate multiple expressions on the same command line. We can use the preceding syntax with AND (`&&`) or OR (`||`) logical operators.

String comparison options for the test command

The following is a summary of various options for string comparison using test, which is taken from the Bash reference manual available at `http://www.gnu.org/software/bash/`:

Test operator	Tests true if
`-n string`	True if the length of string is non-zero.
`-z string`	True if the length of string is zero.
`string1 != string2`	True if the strings are not equal.
`string1 == string2` `string1 = string2`	True if the strings are equal.
`string1 > string2`	True if `string1` sorts after `string2` lexicographically.
`string1 < string2`	True if `string1` sorts before `string2` lexicographically.

If we want to check whether the length of a string is non-zero, then we can check it as follows:

```
test -n $string        or        [ -n $string ]
echo $?
```

If the result is 0, then we can conclude that the string length is non-zero. If the content of ? is non-zero, then the string is 0 in length.

Let's write a shell script, test01.sh, for learning various string operations:

```
#!/bin/bash

str1="Ganesh"
str2="Mumbai";
str3=

[ $str1 = $str2 ] # Will Check Two Strings Are Equal Or Not
echo $?

[ $str1 != $str2 ] # Will Check Two Strings Are Not Equal
echo $?

[ -n $str1 ] # Will confirm string length is greater than zero
echo $?

[ -z $str3 ] # Will Confirm length of String is Zero
echo $?
```

Let's test the following program:

```
$ chmod +x test01.sh
$ ./test01.sh
```

The following will be the output after executing the preceding commands:

```
1
0
0
0
```

Let's write an interactive shell script, test02.sh, to get names from the user and then compare whether both are the same:

```
#!/bin/bash
echo "Enter First name"
```

```
read name1
echo "Enter Second name"
read name2
[ $name1 = $name2 ] # Check equality of two names
echo $?
[ -n  $name2 ] # Check String Length is greater than Zero
echo $?
```

Let's test the following program:

```
$ chmod +x test02.sh
$ ./test02.sh
```

The following will be the output after executing the preceding commands:

```
Enter First name
LEVANA
Enter Second name
TECHNOLOGIES
1
0
```

Numerical comparison operators for the test command

The following is the summary of various options for numerical comparison using `test`:

Test Operator	Tests True If
`[ integer_1 -eq integer_2 ]`	`integer_1` is equal to `integer_2`
`[integer_1 -ne integer_2 ]`	`integer_1` is not equal to `integer_2`
`[integer_1 -gt integer_2 ]`	`integer_1` is greater than `integer_2`
`[integer_1 -ge integer_2 ]`	`integer_1` is greater than or equal to `integer_2`
`[integer_1 -ge integer_2 ]`	`integer_1` is less than `integer_2` .
`[integer_1 -le integer_2 ]`	`integer_1` is less than or equal to `integer_2`

Let's write the shell script, `test03.sh`, for learning the various numerical test operators' usage:

```
#!/bin/bash

num1=10
num2=30

echo $(($num1 < $num2))    # compare for less than
[ $num1 -lt $num2 ]        # compare for less than
echo $?
[ $num1 -ne $num2 ]        # compare for not equal
echo $?
[ $num1 -eq $num2 ]        # compare for equal to
echo $?
```

Let's test the following program:

```
$ chmod +x test03.sh
$ ./test03.sh
```

The following will be the output after executing the preceding commands:

```
1
0
0
1
```

Let's write the script, `test04.sh`, for interactively asking the user for three numbers and then testing those numbers for various comparisons:

```
#!/bin/bash
echo "Please enter 1st First Number"
read num1
echo "Please enter 2nd Number"
read num2
echo "Please enter 3rd Number"
read num3
[[ $num1 > $num2 ]]   # compare for greater than
echo $?
[[ $num1 != $num2 ]] # compare for not equal to
echo $?
[[ $num2 == $num3 ]] # compare for equal to
echo $?
[[ $num1 && $num2 ]] # Logical And Operation
echo $?
[[ $num2 || $num3 ]] # Logical OR Operation
echo $?
```

Let's test the following program:

```
$ chmod +x test04.sh
$ ./test04.sh
```

The following will be the output after executing the preceding commands:

```
Please enter 1st First Number
10
Please enter 2nd Number
20
Please enter 3rd Number
30
1
0
1
0
0
```

Let's write the script test05.sh for using string and numerical test operations:

```
#!/bin/bash
Var1=20
Var2=30
Str1="Accenture"
FileName="TestStringOperator"

test $Var1 -lt $Var2  # Test for Less Than
echo $?
test $Var1 -gt $Var2  # Test For Greater Than
echo $?
test -n $Str1         # Test for String Having Length Greater Than 0
echo $?
test -f $FileName     # Test for File Attributes
echo $?
```

Let's test the following program:

```
$ chmod +x test05.sh
$ ./test05.sh
```

The following will be the output after executing the preceding commands:

```
0
1
0
1
```

We used the test operation for the file in this script. It will check whether the file is present. You will learn more about it in the following section.

Now we will write the script `test06.sh` using the test command interactively, ask the user for data, and then perform numerical, as well as string comparison, operations:

```
#!/bin/bash
echo "Please enter 1st Number"
read num1
echo "Please enter 2nd Number"
read num2
echo
test $num1 -eq $num2     # Test for Equal
echo $?
test $num1 -ne $num2     # Test for Not Equal
echo $?
test $num1 -ge $num2     # Test for Greater Than Equal
echo $?

echo "Please enter 1st String"
read Str1
echo "Please enter 2nd String"
read Str2

test $Str1 = $Str2     # Test for Two Strings Are Equal
echo $?
test -z $Str1          # Test for The Length Of The String Is > 0
echo $?
test $Str2             # Test for The String Is Not NULL
echo $?
```

Let's test the following program:

```
$ chmod +x test06.sh
$ ./test06.sh
```

The following will be the output after executing the preceding commands:

```
Please enter 1st Number
10
Please enter 2nd Number
20
1
0
1
Please enter 1st String
LEVANA
```

```
Please enter 2nd String
TECHNOLOGIES
1
1
0
```

Depending on the value of `$?` in the preceding output, we can decide whether the operation returned `true` or `false`. We will use this in `if`, `case`, and similar decision-making, as well as in looping, activities.

File test options for the test command

The following are the various options for file-handling operations using the test command:

`-c file_name` Check whether file is character special file

`-d file_name` Check whether directory exists

`-e file_name` Check whether file exists

`-f file_name` Check whether file is a regular file and not a directory

`-G file_name` Check whether file exists and is owned by the effective group ID

`-g file_name` Check whether file has `Set-group-ID` set

`-k file_name` Check whether file has `Sticky` bit set

`-L file_name` Check whether file is symbolic link

`-p file_name` Check whether file is a named pipe

`-O file_name` Check whether file exists and is owned by the effective user ID

`-r file_name` Check whether file is readable

`-S file_name` Check whether file is a socket

`-s file_name` Check whether the file has non-zero size

`-t file_name` Check whether the file has `fd` (file descriptor) and is open in a terminal

`-u file_name` Check whether the file has `Set-user-ID` bit set

File-testing binary operators

The following are various options for binary file operations using test, which is taken from the Bash reference manual available at http://www.gnu.org/software/bash/:

Test Operator	Tests True If
[file_1 -nt file_2]	Check whether file_1 is newer than file_2
[file_1 -ot file_2]	Check whether file_1 is older than file_2
[file_1 -ef file_2]	Check whether file_1 and file_2 have the same device or inode numbers

Let's write the script test07.sh to test the basic file attributes, such as whether it is a file or folder and whether it has a file size bigger than 0. The output will be different depending on whether the case file is present:

```
#!/bin/bash
# Check whether file is Directory
[ -d work ]
echo $?
# Check that is it a File
[ -f test.txt ]
echo $?
# Check whether File has size greater than 0
[ -s test.txt ]
echo $?
```

Let us test the program:

```
$ chmod +x test07.sh
$ ./test07.sh
```

The following will be the output after executing the preceding commands:

```
1
1
1
$ mkdir work
$ touch test.txt
$ ./test07.sh
0
0
1
```

We executed the script with and without the directory and `text.txt` file.

The following script, `test08.sh`, is checking the file permissions such as read, write, and execute permissions:

```
#!/bin/bash
# Check whether File has Read Permission
[ -r File2 ]
echo $?
# Check whether File Has Write Permission
[ -w File2 ]
echo $?
# Check whether File Has Execute Permission
[ -x File2 ]
echo $?
```

Let's test the program:

```
$ touch File2
$ ls -l File2
-rw-rw-r-- 1 student student     0 Jun 23 22:37 File2
$ chmod +x test08.sh
$ ./test08.sh
```

The following will be the output after executing the preceding commands:

```
0
0
1
```

Logical test operators

The following are the various options for logical operations using test, which is taken from the Bash reference manual available at `http://www.gnu.org/software/bash/`:

Test Operator	Tests True If
`[ string_1 -a string_1 ]`	Both `string_1` and `string_2` are true
`[ string_1 -o string_2 ]`	Either `string_1` or `string_2` is true
`[ ! string_1 ]`	Not a `string_1` match
`[[ pattern_1 && pattern_2 ]]`	Both `pattern_1` and `pattern_2` are true
`[[ pattern_1 || pattern_2 ]]`	Either `pattern_1` or `pattern_2` is true
`[[ ! pattern ]]`	Not a pattern match

We can use the test operator for strings along with pattern matching as follows:

```
$ name=Ganesh
$ [[ $name == [Gg]anesh ]]        # Wildcards allowed
$ echo $?
0
```

The following is an example for multiple strings with the `&&` logical operator:

```
$ name=Ganesh; friend=Anil
$ [[ $name == [Gg]anesh && $friend == "Lydia" ]]
$ echo $?
1
```

The following is the script with the test command along with the extended pattern matching enabled:

```
$ shopt -s extglob        # we are enabling extended pattern matching
$ city=Kannur
$ [[ $city == [Kk]a+(n)ur ]]
$ echo $?
0
```

In the given expressions, we are checking the equality of strings. It tests whether the city name starts with K or k, followed by a, one or more n characters, u, and r.

Conditional constructs – if else

We use the `if` expression to check the pattern or command status and accordingly we can make certain decisions to execute scripts or commands.

The syntax of the `if` conditional is as follows:

```
if      command
then
    command
    command
fi
```

From the preceding syntax, we can clearly understand the working of the if conditional construct. Initially, if will execute the command. If the result of command execution is true or 0, then all the commands that are enclosed between then and fi will be executed. If the status of command execution after if is false or non-zero, then all the commands after then will be ignored and the control of execution will directly go to fi.

Let's learn another variation of if constructs.

Syntax:

```
if command
then
      command
      command
else
      command
fi
```

In the preceding case, if the command after if is successfully executed or the status variable ? content is 0, then all the commands after then will be executed. If the result of the command is a failure or non-zero, then all the commands after else will be executed.

For numeric or string expression evaluations using if, the syntax is as follows:

```
if [ string/numeric expression ]
then
     command
fi
```

Alternatively, use the following syntax:

```
if [[ string expression ]]
then
     command
fi
```

Alternatively, use the following syntax:

```
if (( numeric expression ))
then
     command
fi
```

A simple example of checking the status of the last command executed using the `if` construct is as follows:

```
#!/bin/bash
if [ $? -eq 0 ]
then
        echo "Command was successful."
else
        echo "Command was successful."
fi
```

Whenever we run any command, the exit status of the command will be stored in the ? variable. The preceding construct will be very useful in checking the status of the last command.

Numerical handling if constructs

Let's learn about using the `if` construct for numerical decision-making.

We can use the `test` command for finding which variable contains the smaller value:

```
$ X=10
$ y=20
$ (( x < y ))
$ echo $?
0
The result 0 shows that x is smaller than y.
```

In the shell script `if_01.sh`, we can use the `test` command along with the `if` construct for checking the equality of variables with numerical values as follows:

```
#!/bin/bash
a=100
if [ $a -eq 100 ]
then
    echo "a is equal to $a"
else
        echo "a is not equal"
fi
```

Let's test the following program:

```
$ chmod +x if_01.sh
$ ./if_01.sh
```

The following will be the output after executing the preceding commands:

```
a is equal to 100
```

Use the script if_02.sh to check which product is costly. The script is as follows:

```
#!/bin/bash
echo "Enter the cost of product a"
read a
echo "Enter the cost of product b"
read b

if [ $a -gt $b ]
then
 echo " a is greater"
else
 echo " b is greater"
fi
```

Let's test the following program:

```
$ chmod +x if_02.sh
$ ./if_02.sh
```

The following will be the output after executing the preceding commands:

```
Enter the cost of product a
100
Enter the cost of product b
150
 b is greater
$
```

Using the exit command and the ? variable

If we need to terminate the shell script and come back to the command line, then we can use the exit command. The syntax is very simple:

```
exit 0
```

The given command will terminate the shell script and return to the command line. It will store the 0 value in the ? status variable. We can use any value between 0 and 255. Value 0 means success, and any other non-zero value means an error. We can use these values to indicate error information.

The script to check the value of a parameter that is passed along with the command (either less than 0 or greater than 30) is as follows. This will save us from using the nested if statement:

```
#!/bin/bash
if (( $1 <  0 || $1 > 30 ))
    then
        echo "mdays is out of range"
        exit 2
fi
```

The test command used in the preceding expression for OR can be written as follows:

```
[ $1 -lt 0 -o $1 -gt 30 ]
```

String handling with the if construct

Let's learn about using string-related checking using the if expression.

The following script, if_03.sh, will check the equality of two strings:

```
echo "Enter the first string to compare"
read name1
echo "Enter the Second string to compare"
read name2

if [  "$name1" == "$name2" ]
then
    echo "First string is equal to Second string"
else
    echo "Strings are not same"
fi
```

Let's test the following program:

```
$ chmod +x if_03.sh
$ ./if_03.sh
```

The following will be the output after executing the preceding commands:

```
$ ./ if_03.sh
Enter the first string to compare
LEVANA
Enter the Second string to compare
TECHNOLOGIES
Strings are not same
$ ./ if_03.sh
```

The following will be the output after executing the preceding commands:

```
Enter the first string to compare
LEVANA
Enter the Second string to compare
LEVANA
First string is equal to Second string
$
```

We will write the script for performing various other string operations using a test. Let's write the script if_04.sh to compare two strings for various attributes:

```
#!/bin/bash

str1="Ganesh"
str2="Naik"

if [ $str1 = $str2 ]
then
    echo "Two Strings Are Equal"
fi

if [ $str1 != $str2 ]
then
    echo "Two Strings are not equal"
fi

if [ $str1 ]
then
    echo "String One Has Size Greater Than Zero"
fi

if [ $str2 ]
```

```
then
    echo "String Two Has Size Greater Than Zero"
fi
```

Let's test the following program:

```
$ chmod +x if_04.sh
$ ./if_04.sh
```

The following will be the output after executing the preceding commands:

```
Two Strings are not equal
String One Has Size Greater Than Zero
String Two Has Size Greater Than Zero
```

If we want to verify whether the entered password is valid, then script if_05.sh will be as follows:

```
#!/bin/bash
stty -echo          # password will not be printed on screen
read -p "Please enter a password  :" password
if test "$password" == "Abrakadabra"
then
echo "Password is matching"
fi
stty echo
```

Let's test the following program:

```
$ chmod +x if_05.sh
$ ./if_05.sh
```

The following will be the output after executing the preceding commands:

```
$ ./if_05.sh
Please enter a password  :  levana
$ ./if_05.sh
Please enter a password  : Abrakadabra
Password is matching
$
```

Checking for null values

Many a time we need to check the value of variable, such as whether it is null. The null value means zero value. If we want to create the string with the null value, then we should use double quotes ("") while declaring it:

```
if [ "$string" = "" ]
then
echo "The string is null"
fi
```

We can even use [! "$string"] or [-z "$string"] for null checking of strings.

Let's write the script if_08.sh, which will search for the entered person's name and tell us whether the user is on the computer system:

```
#!/bin/bash
read -p "Enter a user name : " user_name

# try to locate username in in /etc/passwd
#
grep "^$user_name" /etc/passwd > /dev/null

status=$?

if test $status -eq 0
then
    echo "User '$user_name' is found in /etc/passwd."
else
    echo "User '$user_name' is not found in /etc/passwd."
fi
```

Let's test the following program:

```
$ chmod +x if_08.sh
$ ./if_08.sh
```

The following will be the output after executing the preceding commands:

```
Enter a user name : ganesh
User 'ganesh' is not found in /etc/passwd.
```

In the preceding script, we are searching for the username in the /etc/passwd file. If a person's name is not found in the /etc/passwd file, then we can conclude that the username has not been created in the system.

Let's write a script to check the disk space being used. The script will print a warning if 90 percent or more of the disk space is used on one of the mounted partitions.

The shell script `if_09.sh` for solving the disk filesystem usage warning will be as follows:

```
#!/bin/bash
df -h | grep /dev/sda1 | cut -c 35-36 > log.txt
read usage < log.txt
if [ $usage -gt 80 ]
then
    echo "Warning - Disk file system has exceeded 80% !"
    echo "Please move extra data to backup device."
else
    echo "Good - You have enough disk space to continue working !"
fi
```

Let's test the following program:

```
$ chmod +x if_09.sh
$ ./if_09.sh
```

If the preceding program does not work, due to some hardware differences, then make the following changes to the script:

1. Check to see whether your partition for storage is sda1, sda2, or any other by entering the $df -h command.
2. Check whether the % disk utilization value is at character count 35 and 36. If not, then make changes in the code accordingly.

Using the df command, we get the disk filesystem usage information. The grep command is filtering the hard disk partition, which contains our data. Then, we filter the disc % utilization number and store that value in the log.txt file. Using the read command, we read the % utilization and store it in the usage variable. Later on, using the if command, we check and warn the user if the % utilization is greater than 80.

File handling with the if command

You have already learned about how to use the test command for checking various file operations such as checking the file's permissions and similar other attributes. A command's task in any script is to check whether the file or folder is present or not. Then, accordingly, we need to proceed. We will see how to use the if command along with the test command.

Use the simple script `if_10.sh` to check whether the file exists or not in the current directory as follows:

```
#!/bin/bash
read filename
if test -e $filename
then
    echo "file exists"
else
    echo " file does not exist"
fi
```

Let's test the program as follows:

```
$ chmod +x if_10.sh
$ ./if_10.sh
```

The following will be the output after executing the preceding commands:

```
sample.txt
file does not exist
$ touch sample.txt
$ ./if_10.sh
sample.txt
file exists
```

First, we checked without the file. Then, we created a file with the `touch` command. We can very easily check for the presence of the file.

Let's learn how to use the `if` command to check various file attributes, such as whether it exists, whether it has file permissions to read, write, execute, and similar by writing script `if_11.sh` as follows:

```
#!/bin/bash
echo "$1 is: "
if ! [ -e $1 ]
then
  echo "..Do not exists"
  exit
else
  echo "file is present"
fi

if [ -x $1 ]
then
  echo "..Executable"
fi
```

```
if [ -r $1 ]
then
  echo "..Readable"
fi

if [ -w $1 ]
then
  echo "..Writable"
fi
```

Let's test the following program:

```
$ chmod +x if_11.sh
$ ./if_11.sh sample.txt
```

This should be the output:

```
sample.txt is:
"file is present"
..Readable
..Writable
```

The shell script if_12.sh for performing the file copy operation and then checking whether the copy operation was successful will be as follows:

```
#!/bin/bash
file1="File1"
file2="File2"
if cp $file1 $file2
then
  echo "Copy Command Executed Successfully"
  echo "Content of file named Fil1 copied in another file named File2"
else
  echo "Some problem in command execution"
fi
```

Let's test the program:

```
$ chmod +x if_12.sh
$ ./if_12.sh
```

The following will be the output after executing the preceding commands:

```
$ touch File1
$ ./if_12.sh
Copy Command Executed Successfully
Content of file named Fil1 copied in another file named File2
```

Multiple test commands and if constructs

These type of constructs enable us to execute the second command depending on the success or failure of the first command:

```
command1      &&      command2
command1      ||      command2
```

Let's write script if_13.sh. In this script, we will ask the user to input two numbers. Then, the if statement will evaluate two expressions. If both are true, then the command after then will be executed; otherwise, commands after else will be called:

```
#!/bin/bash
echo "Enter the first number"
read val_a
echo "Enter the Second number"
read val_b

if [ $val_a == 1 ] && [ $val_b == 10 ]
then
  echo "testing is successful"
else
  echo "testing is not successful"
fi
```

Let's test the program:

```
$ chmod +x if_13.sh
$ ./if_13.sh
```

The following will be the output after executing the preceding commands:

```
Enter the first number
10
Enter the Second number
20
testing is not successful
$ ./if_13.sh
Enter the first number
1
Enter the Second number
10
testing is successful
```

Sometimes, we may need to enter a command to check whether the file has the execute permission ? If it is executable, then the file should be executed. The script for such a requirement will be as follows:

```
test -e file &&  .  file.
```

Let's learn one more example of && and multiple expressions using the test command. In the following script, if_14.sh, we will check whether file_one is present, then we will print Hello and then immediately we will check whether file_two is present. Then we will print there on the screen:

```
#!/bin/bash

touch file_one
touch file_two

if [ -f "file_one" ] && echo "Hello" && [ -f file_two ] && echo  "there"
then
   echo  "in if"
else
   echo     "in else"
fi
exit 0
```

Let's test the program:

```
$ chmod +x if_14.sh
$ ./if_14.sh
```

The following will be the output after executing the preceding commands:

```
Hello
there
in if
```

The following script, if_15.sh, will check file permissions such as read, write, and execute in the same if command using multiple && with the test command:

```
#!/bin/bash
echo "Please enter file name for checking file permissions"
read file
if [[ -r $file && -w $file && -x $file ]]
then
     echo "The file has read, write,and execute permission"
fi
```

Let's test the program:

```
$ chmod +x if_15.sh
$ touch sample.txt
$ chmod +rwx sample.txt
$ ./if_15.sh
sample.txt
```

The following will be the output after executing the preceding commands:

```
The file has read, write, and execute permissions.
```

Till now, we have seen multiple expressions using the && logical operator. Now we will see one example with the OR (| |) logical operator. In the following script, if_16.sh, we will check the existence of file_one and then we will print Hello on the screen. If the first expression of file checking fails, then the second expression of echo will be executed:

```
#!/bin/sh
if [ -f file_one ] || echo "Hello"
then
    echo "In if"
else
    echo "In else"
fi
```

Let's test the program:

```
$ chmod +x if_16.sh
$ ./if_16.sh
```

The following will be the output after executing the preceding commands:

```
hello
In if
$ touch file_one
$ ./if_16.sh
```

This is the output:

```
In if
```

We checked in the preceding script whether file_one is absent or present.

The if/elif/else command

Sometimes, we need to make a decision on multiple situations or options, such as whether a city is the capital of a country, the state capital, a major city, or a small town. In such situations where, depending on various options, we need to execute different commands, `if/else` or `if/elif/else` decision-making commands are useful.

Using the `if/elif/else` commands, we can have multiple decision-making processes. If the `if` command succeeds, the command after `then` will be executed. If it fails, the command after the `elif` statement will be tested. If that statement succeeds, then statements under the `elif` are executed. However, suppose none of the `elif` conditions are true, then statements after the `else` command are executed. Here, the `else` block is executed by default. The `fi` statement will close the `if/elif/else` command.

The syntax of decision-making using the `if elif` construct is as follows:

```
If      expression_1
then
    Command

elif
    expression_2
then
    Command

elif
    expression_3
then
    Command

else
  Command

    fi
```

Let's write script `if_18.sh` as follows. In this script, we are checking whether the directory with a given name exists or not. If this fails, then we are checking whether the file with the given name exists. Even if this fails, then we will inform the user that neither the file nor the directory exists with the given name:

```
#!/bin/bash
echo "Kindly enter name of directory : "
read file

if [[ -d $file ]]
```

```
then
        echo "$file is a directory"
elif [[ -f $file ]]
    then
    echo "$file is a file."
 else
        echo "$file is neither a file nor a directory. "
fi
```

Let's test the program:

```
$ chmod +x if_18.sh
$ ./if_18.sh
```

The following will be the output after executing the preceding commands:

```
$ ./if_18.sh
Kindly enter name of directory :
File1
File1 is a file.
$ mkdir dir1
$ ./if_18.sh
Kindly enter name of directory :
dir1
dir1 is a directory
$ ./if_18.sh
Kindly enter name of directory :
File007
File007 is neither a file nor a directory.
```

The null command

In many situations, we may need a command that does nothing and returns a success status such as 0. In such cases, we can use the null command. It is represented by a colon (:). For example, in the if loop, we do not want to add any command if it is successful, but we have certain commands to execute if it fails. In such situations, we can use the null command. This is illustrated in the following if_19.sh script. If we want to loop for ever, then the null command can be used in the for loop:

```
#!/bin/bash
city=London
if grep "$city" city_database_file >& /dev/null
then
        :
else
```

```
        echo "City is not found in city_database_file "
        exit 1
  fi
```

Let's test the program:

```
    $ chmod +x if_19.sh
    $ ./if_19.sh
```

The following will be the output after executing the preceding commands:

```
    City is not found in city_database_file
```

We can observe from the preceding script that the colon is a `null` command and it does nothing.

Switching case

Apart from simple branches with `if`, it is also possible to process multiple decision-making operations using the `case` command. In a `case` statement, the expression contained in a variable is compared with a number of expressions, and for each expression matched, a command is executed.

It is possible to have multiple branches using the `if/elif/else` commands. But if more than two or three `elif` commands are used, then code becomes very complex. When all the different conditions are depending on a single variable, in such cases, the `esac` statement is used. The interpreter checks the value of the `case` variable against `value1`, `value2`, `value3`, and so on, till the match is found. If the value is matched, then all the statements after that `case` value are executed till the double semicolon is reached. If nothing is matched, then statements after `esac` are executed. Wildcard characters and pipes (vertical bar for *ORing* two values) are allowed in the `case` statement.

A `case` statement has the following structure:

```
case variable in
  value1)
    command(s)
    ;;
  value2)
    command(s)
    ;;
  *)
    command(s)
```

```
        ;;
esac
```

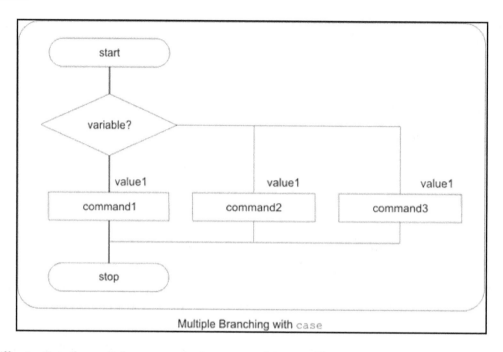

Multiple Branching with case

For illustrating the switch `case` scripting example, we will write the `case_01.sh` script as follows. We will ask the user to enter any number from the range `1-9`. We will check the entered number with the `case` command. If a user enters any other number, then we will display the error by displaying the `Invalid key` message:

```bash
#!/bin/bash

echo "Please enter any number from 1 to 9"
read number

case $number in
  1) echo "ONE"
    ;;
  2) echo "TWO"
    ;;
  3) echo "Three"
    ;;
  4) echo "FOUR"
     ;;
  5) echo "FIVE"
    ;;
```

```
6) echo "SIX"
   ;;
7) echo "SEVEN"
   ;;
8) echo "EIGHT"
   ;;
9) echo "NINE"
   ;;
*) echo "SOME ANOTHER NUMBER"
   ;;
esac
```

Let's test the program:

```
$ chmod +x case_01.sh
$ ./case_01.sh
```

The following will be the output after executing the preceding commands:

```
Please enter any number from 1 to 9
5
FIVE
```

Sometimes, in the shell script we may need to ask for an email address from the user. In such situations, we need to verify whether the address is correct. We can use the case command to validate the correct email address as follows:

```
#!/bin/bash
case $1  in
*@*.com)   echo "valid email address"
    ;;
*)    echo "invalid string"
    ;;
esac
```

Let's test the program:

```
$ chmod +x case_02..sh
$ ./case_02.sh   abc@gmail.com
```

The following will be the output after executing the preceding commands if the email address is correct:

```
valid email address
$ ./case_02.sh abc.com
```

The following will be the output after executing the preceding commands if the email address is not correct:

```
invalid string
```

If, inside the script we need to provide file operations such as copy, move, or delete, then we can use the case command for such scripts. The script case_03.sh for file operations is as follows:

```
#!/bin/bash
echo "Press 1 for copy or 2 for move or 3 for removing the file"
read num
case $num in
1)   echo "We are going to do copy operation"
echo " Enter Source file name"
read source
echo " Enter destination file name"
read destination
cp $source $destination
;;
2)   echo "We are going to do move operation"
echo " Enter Source file name"
read source
echo "Enter destination file name"
read destination
mv $source $destination   ;;
3)   echo "We are going to remove the file"
echo " Enter the name of file to remove"
read source
rm $source   ;;
*) echo "invalid key"
esac
```

Let's test the program:

```
$ chmod +x case_03.sh
$ ./case_03.sh
```

The following will be the output after executing the preceding commands:

```
Press 1 for copy or 2 for move or 3 for removing the file
1
We are going to do copy operation
 Enter Source file name
File1
 Enter destination file name
File4
```

In this shell script `case_04.sh`, we will ask the user to enter the day of the week. Inside the script, we will detect the text entered and print a detailed description of the day such as `First Day is Monday` and similar on the screen. Note that we are able to perform pattern matching for the uppercase and lowercase in the `case` statement:

```bash
#!/bin/bash
echo "Enter Day Of The Week"
read day

case $day in
  [mM][oO][nN][dD][aA][yY])
        echo "First Day is Monday"
        ;;
  [tT][uU][eE][sS][dD][aA][yY])
        echo "Second Day Tuesday"
        ;;
  [wW][eE][dD][nN][eE][sS][dD][aA][yY])
        echo "Third Day Wednesday"
        ;;
  [tT][hH][uU][rR][sS][dD][aA][yY])
        echo " Fourth Day Thursday"
        ;;
  [fF][rR][iI][dD][aA][yY])
        echo "Fifth Day Friday"
        ;;
  [sS][aA][tT][uU][rR][dD][aA][yY])
        echo "Sixth Day Saturday"
        ;;
  [sS][uU][nN][dD][aA][yY])
        echo "Seventh Day Sunday"
        ;;
  *)
    echo "Invalid Day of Week"
    ;;
  esac
```

Let's test the program:

```
$ chmod +x case_04.sh
$ ./case_04.sh
```

The following will be the output after executing the preceding commands:

```
$ ./case_04.sh
Enter Day Of The Week
Monday
First Day is Monday
$ ./case_04.sh
Enter Day Of The Week
Thursday
Fourth Day Thursday
```

We write the script case_05.sh for printing days in the current month. We will use the date command in the script for finding the current month:

```
#!/bin/bash
mth=$(date +%m)

case $mth in
02)
  echo "February usually has 28 days."
  echo "If it is a leap year, it has 29 days."
  ;;

04|06|09|11)
  echo "The current month has 30 days."
  ;;

*)
  echo "The current month has 31 days."
  ;;
 esac
```

Let's test the program:

```
$ chmod +x case_05.sh
$ ./case_05.sh
```

The following will be the output after executing the preceding commands:

```
The current month has 30 days.
```

Implementing simple menus with select

With the Bash shell, it is possible to create simple menus with the help of the built-in `select` command.

The syntax of `select` is as follows:

```
PS3=prompting-text
select VARIABLE in item1 item2 item3
do
   commands
done
```

The advantage of a menu with `select` is that we can have an endless loop with it. We can have a condition in which we exit the loop.

In the following script, `select_01.sh`, we show the menu with five options including a, bc, def, ghi, and jkl. The script will execute the command inside `do` and `done`:

```
#!/bin/bash
select var1 in a   bc    def     ghi     jkl
do
echo "Present value of var1 is $var1
done
```

Let's test the program:

```
$ chmod +x select_01.sh
$ ./select_01.sh
```

The following will be the output after executing the preceding commands:

```
1) a
2) bc
3) def
4) ghi
5) jkl
#? 2
"Present value of var1 is bc
#? 4
"Present value of var1 is ghi
#? 5
"Present value of var1 is jkl
#?
Press    ^C    to quit
```

We can implement the `case` command inside the `do` and `done` part of the `select` menu. The syntax will be as follows:

```
PS3=prompting text
select   VARIABLE in  item1   item2 item3
do
  case VARIABLE in
  value1 ) command1 ; ;
  value2 ) command2 ; ;
esac
done
```

In the following script, `select_02.sh`, we used the `case` command inside `do` and `done`. This gives us many convenient features. Due to `select`, we get endless such as continuous loop. In case the `if` option entered is `quit`, then it exits the continuous loop:

```
#!/bin/bash
PS3="please  select any one : "
select var in a b quit
do
case $var in
  a) echo option is a ;;
  b) echo option is b ;;
  quit) exit ;;
  *) echo option is default ;;
esac
done
```

Let's test the program:

```
$ chmod +x select_02.sh
$ ./select_02.sh
```

The following will be the output after executing the preceding commands:

```
1) a
2) b
3) quit
please  select any one : 1
option is a
please  select any one : 2
option is b
please  select any one : 3
```

In the following script, `select_03.sh`, we use a `case` statement with numerical options 1, 2, 3, 4, and an option for an invalid choice:

```
#!/bin/bash
PS3="Please enter one of the option"
select var in 1 2 3 4
do
case $var in
    1) echo "One is selected";;
    2) echo "Two is selected";;
    3) echo "Two is selected";;
    4) echo "Two is selected";;
    *) echo "not a proper option";;
esac
done
```

Let's test the program:

```
$ chmod +x select_03.sh
$ ./select_03.sh
```

The following will be the output after executing the preceding commands:

```
1) 1
2) 2
3) 3
4) 4
Please enter one of the option : 1
"One is selected"
Please enter one of the option : 2
"Two is selected
Please enter one of the option : 3
"Three is selected
Please enter one of the option : 4
"Four is selected
Please enter one of the option : 8
"not a proper option"
Please enter one of the option :
```

In the `case` statement, we can add many choices to select the same command. Here is an example of the script `select_04.sh` as follows:

```
#!/bin/bash
PS3="Please select one of the above:"
select COMPONENT in comp1 comp2 comp3 all none
do
case $COMPONENT in
```

```
comp1|comp2|comp3) echo "comp1 or comp2 co comp3 selected" ;;
all) echo "selected all"
;;
none) break ;;
*) echo "ERROR: Invalid selection, $REPLY." ;;
esac
done
```

Let's test the program:

```
$ chmod +x select_04.sh
$ ./select_04.sh
```

The following will be the output after executing the preceding commands:

```
1) comp1
2) comp2
3) comp3
4) all
5) none
Please select one of the above:
```

The script `select_05.sh` is used to inform the user about calorie information in fruits, as follows:

```
#!/bin/bash
PS3="Enter the number for your fruit choice: "

select fruit in apple orange banana peach pear "Quit Menu"
do
  case $fruit in
    apple)
      echo "An apple has 80 calories."
      ;;

    orange)
      echo "An orange has 65 calories."
      ;;

    banana)
      echo "A banana has 100 calories."
      ;;

    peach)
      echo "A peach has 38 calories."
      ;;

    pear)
```

```
      echo "A pear has 100 calories."
      ;;

   "Quit Menu")
      break
      ;;

   *)
      echo "You did not enter a correct choice."
      ;;
 esac
done
```

Let's test the program:

```
$ chmod +x select_05.sh
$ ./select_05.sh
```

The following will be the output after executing the preceding commands:

```
1) apple      3) banana      5) pear
2) orange     4) peach       6) Quit Menu
Enter the number for your fruit choice: 1
An apple has 80 calories.
Enter the number for your fruit choice: 2
An orange has 65 calories.
Enter the number for your fruit choice: 3
A banana has 100 calories.
Enter the number for your fruit choice: 4
A peach has 38 calories.
Enter the number for your fruit choice: 5
A pear has 100 calories.
Enter the number for your fruit choice: 6
```

Summary

In this chapter, you learned about using decision-making in scripts by working with Test, if-else, and switching case. We also learned how to implement simple menus with select.

In the next chapter, you will learn about looping in scripts by working with For, While, and until loops. You will also learn how to control loops using the break statement and continue statement.

Automating Repetitive Tasks

9

In the previous chapter, you learned about using decision making in scripts by working with `Test`, `if-else`, and switching `case`. You also learned how to implement simple menus with select.

In this chapter, we will cover the following topics:

- Working with the `for` loop
- Working with the `while` loop
- Controlling loops:
  - The `continue` statement
  - The `break` statement

Looping with the for command

For iterative operations, the `bash` shell uses three types of loops: `for`, `while`, and `until`. Using the `for` looping command, we can execute a set of commands for a finite number of times for every item in a list. In the `for` loop command, the user-defined variable is specified. After the `in` command, the keyword list of values can be specified. The user-defined variable will get the value from that list, and all statements between `do` and `done` get executed until it reaches the end of the list.

The purpose of the `for` loop is to process a list of elements. It has the following syntax:

```
for variable in element1 element2 element3
do
commands
done
```

The simple script with the `for` loop could be as follows:

```
for command in clear date cal
do
   sleep 1
   $command
Done
```

In the preceding script, the commands `clear`, `date`, and `cal` will be called one after another. The `sleep` command will be called before every command for one second.

If we need to loop continuously or infinitely, then the following is the syntax:

```
for ((;;))
do
     command
done
```

Let's write a simple `for_01.sh` script. In this script, we will print the `var` variable 10 times:

```
#!/bin/bash
for var in {1..10}
do
   echo $var
done
```

Let's test the program:

```
$ chmod +x for_01.sh
$ ./for_01.sh
```

The following will be the output after executing the preceding commands:

```
1
2
3
4
5
6
7
8
9
10
```

The following `for_02.sh` script uses the C programming style syntax:

```
#!/bin/bash
max=10
for  ((i=1; i<=max;  i++))
do
echo -n "$i      "    # one case with echo without -n option
done
```

Let's test the program:

```
$ chmod +x for_02.sh
$ ./for_02.sh
```

The following will be the output after executing the preceding commands:

```
$ ./for_02.sh        # OUTPUT with -n option
1      2      3      4      5      6      7      8      9      10
$ ./for_02.sh        # OUTPUT without -n option
1
2
3
4
5
6
7
8
9
10
```

In the next `for_03.sh` script, we will be processing a list of numbers, which are listed next to the in keyword:

```
#!/bin/bash
for var in 11 12 13 14 15 16 17 18 19 20
do
  echo $var
done
```

Let's test the program:

```
$ chmod +x for_03.sh
$ ./for_03.sh
```

The following will be the output after executing the preceding commands:

```
$ ./for_03.sh
11
12
13
14
15
16
17
18
19
20
```

In the following `for_04.sh` script, we create `user11` to `user20`, along with their home directory:

```
#!/bin/bash
for var in user{11..20}
do
  useradd -m $var
  passwd -d $var
done
```

Let's test the program:

```
$ chmod +x for_04.sh
$ sudo ./for_04.sh
```

After executing the preceding command, `user11` to `user20` will be created with their home folders in the `/home/` folder.
You need to be a root user or administrator to run this script.

In the `for_05.sh` script, we will be passing command-line parameters. All the command-line parameters will be available as the `$*` inside script:

```
#!/bin/sh
for var in $*
do
  echo "command line contains: $var"
done
```

Let's test the program:

```
$ chmod +x for_05.sh
$ ./for_05.sh 1 2 3 4 5 6
```

The following will be the output after executing the preceding commands:

```
command line contains: 1
command line contains: 2
command line contains: 3
command line contains: 4
command line contains: 5
command line contains: 6
```

In the next `for_06.sh` script, we are passing a list of words, such as the names of fruits. Inside the script, we are printing the information of the variable:

```
#!/bin/bash
# create fruits.txt => Apple Mango Grapes Pears Banana Orange Pineapple
for var in `cat fruits.txt`
do
    echo "var contains: $var"
done
```

Let's test the program:

```
$ chmod +x for_06.sh
$ ./for_06.sh
```

The following will be the output after executing the preceding commands:

```
var contains: Apple
var contains: Mango
var contains: Grapes
var contains: Pears
var contains: Banana
var contains: Orange
var contains: Pineapple
```

Using the `for_07.sh` script, we generate a list of files with the `ls` shell command. This will be the list of filenames. In the `for` loop, the following list of files will be printed:

```
#!/bin/bash
echo -n "Commands in bin directory are : $var"
for var in $(ls /bin/*)
do
        echo -n -e "$var t"
done
```

Let's test the program:

```
$ chmod +x for_07.sh
$ ./for_07
```

The following will be the output after executing the preceding commands:

```
This will print the content of /bin/ directory.
```

For taking a backup of the files, we can write the `for_08.sh` script as follows:

```
#!/bin/bash
for filename in *.c
do
  echo "Copying $filename to $filename.bak"
  cp $filename $filename.bak
done
```

Let's test the program:

```
$ chmod +x for_08.sh
$ touch 1.c 2.c
$ ./for_08.sh
```

The following will be the output after executing the preceding commands:

```
"Copying 1.c to 1.c.bak"
"Copying 2.c to 2.c.bak"
```

Exiting from the current loop iteration with the continue command

Using the `continue` command, it is possible to exit from the current iteration of the loop and resume the next iteration of the loop. We use the `for`, `while`, or `until` commands for loop iterations.

The following is the `for_09.sh` script for the loop with the `continue` command to skip a certain part of the loop commands:

```
#!/bin/bash
for x in 1 2 3
do
    echo before $x
    continue 1
    echo after $x
done
exit 0
```

Let's test the program:

```
$ chmod +x for_09.sh
$ ./for_09.sh
```

The following will be the output after executing the preceding commands:

```
before 1
before 2
before 3
```

The following is the for_10.sh script in which we will check all files and directories. If the file is found, we will print the name. If the directory is found, we will skip further processing with the continue command. Take care that any of your useful files with the name sample* are not in the testing directory before testing this script:

```
#!/bin/bash
rm -rf sample*
echo > sample_1
echo > sample_2
mkdir sample_3
echo > sample_4

for file in sample*
do
  if [ -d "$file" ]
  then
    echo "skipping directory $file"
    continue
  fi
  echo file is $file
done
rm -rf sample*
exit 0
```

Let's test the program:

```
$ chmod +x for_10.sh
$ ./for_10.sh
```

The following will be the output after executing the preceding commands:

```
file is sample_1
file is sample_2
skipping directory sample_3
file is sample_4
```

In the following `for_11.sh` script, we are checking the backup of files in the /MP3/ folder. If the file is not found in the folder, we are copying it to the folder for backup purposes. We can implement incremental backup scripts using this functionality:

```bash
#!/bin/bash
for    FILE in 'ls *.mp3'
do
  if  test -e /MP3/$FILE
  then
    echo "The file $FILE exists."
    continue
  fi
  cp $FILE /MP3
done
```

Let's test the program:

```
$ chmod +x for_11.sh
$ ./for_11.sh
```

If the file exists in the MP3 folder, then the loop will continue to check the next file. If the file backup is not present in the MP3 folder, then the file will be copied to it.

Exiting from a loop with a break

In the previous section, we discussed about how `continue` can be used to exit from the current iteration of a loop. The `break` command is another way to introduce a new condition within a loop. Unlike `continue`, however, it causes the loop to be terminated altogether if the condition is met.

In the `for_12.sh` script, we check the directory's content. If the directory is found, then we are exiting the loop and displaying the message that the first directory is found:

```bash
#!/bin/bash
rm -rf sample*
echo > sample_1
echo > sample_2
mkdir sample_3
echo > sample_4

for file in sample*
do
  if [ -d "$file" ]; then
    break;
```

```
   fi
done

echo The first directory is $file
rm -rf sample*
exit 0
```

Let's test the program, as follows:

```
$ chmod +x for_12.sh
$ ./for_12.sh
```

The following will be the output after executing the preceding commands:

The first directory is sample_3

In the for_13.sh script, we ask the user to enter any number. We print the square of the numbers in the while loop. If a user enters the number 0, then we use the break command to exit the loop:

```
#!/bin/bash
typeset -i  num=0
while true
do
   echo -n "Enter any number (0 to exit): "
   read num junk

   if (( num == 0 ))
   then
     break
   else
     echo "Square of $num is $(( num * num ))."
   fi
done

echo "script has ended"
```

Let's test the program:

```
$ chmod +x for_13.sh
$ ./for_13.sh
```

The following will be the output after executing the preceding commands:

```
Enter any number (0 to exit): 1
Square of 1 is 1.
Enter any number (0 to exit): 5
Square of 5 is 25.
Enter any number (0 to exit): 0
```

Working with the do – while loop

Similar to the `for` command, `while` is also the command for loop operations. The command next to `while` is evaluated. If it is successful or 0, then the commands inside `do` and `done` are executed.

The purpose of a loop is to test a certain condition or expression and execute a given command `while` the condition is true (the `while` loop) or `until` the condition becomes true (the `until` loop):

```
while condition    until condition
do                 do
commands           commands
done               done
```

The following is the `while_01.sh` script in which we read a file and display its content:

```
#!/bin/bash
file=/etc/resolv.conf
while IFS= read -r line    # IFS : inter field separator
do
    # echo line is stored in $line
  echo $line
done < "$file"
```

Let's test the program:

```
$ chmod +x while_01.sh
$ ./while_01.sh
```

The following will be the output after executing the preceding commands:

```
nameserver 192.168.168.2
search localdomain
```

In the following `while_02.sh` script, we are printing numbers 1–10 on the screen using the `while` loop:

```
#!/bin/bash
declare -i x
x=0
while [ $x -le 10 ]
do
   echo $x
   x=$((x+1))
done
```

Let's test the program:

```
$ chmod +x while_02.sh
$ ./while_02.sh
```

The following will be the output after executing the preceding commands:

```
0
1
2
3
4
5
6
7
8
9
10
```

In the following `while_03.sh` script, we ask the user to input the test. If the input of the text is `quit`, then we terminate the loop; otherwise, we print the text on the screen:

```
#!/bin/bash
INPUT=""
while [ "$INPUT" != quit ]
do
    echo ""
    echo 'Enter a word (quit to exit) : '
    read INPUT
    echo "You typed : $INPUT"
done
```

Let's test the program:

```
$ chmod +x while_03.sh
$ ./while_03.sh
```

The following will be the output after executing the preceding commands:

```
Enter a word (quit to exit) :
GANESH
You typed : GANESH
Enter a word (quit to exit) :
Naik
You typed : Naik
Enter a word (quit to exit) :
quit
You typed : quit
```

In the following while_04.sh script, we print the content of variable num on screen. We are starting with the value of 1. In the loop, we increment the value of the num variable by 1. When the value of the variable num reaches 6, then the while loop is terminated:

```
#!/bin/bash
num=1
while (( num < 6 ))
do
   echo "The value of num is: $num"
   (( num = num + 1 ))                  # let num=num+1
done
echo "Done."
```

Let's test the program:

```
$ chmod +x while_04.sh
$ ./while_04.sh
```

The following will be the output after executing the preceding commands:

```
The value of num is: 1
The value of num is: 2
The value of num is: 3
The value of num is: 4
The value of num is: 5
Done.
```

The `while_05.sh` script prints a series of odd numbers on screen. We are passing a total number of odd numbers required as command-line parameters:

```
#!/bin/bash
count=1
num=1
while [ $count -le $1 ]
do
   echo $num
   num=`expr $num + 2`
   count=`expr $count + 1`
done
```

Let's test the program:

```
$ chmod +x while_05.sh
$ ./while_05.sh 5
```

The following will be the output after executing the preceding commands:

```
1
3
5
7
9
```

Using until

The `until` command is similar to the `while` command. The given statements in the loop are executed as long as they evaluate the condition as true. As soon as the condition becomes false, then the loop is exited.

The syntax is as follows:

```
until command
do
    command(s)
done
```

In the following `until_01.sh` script, we are printing the numbers 0-9 on screen. When the value of variable x becomes 10, then the `until` loop stops executing:

```
#!/bin/bash
x=0
until [ $x -eq 10 ]
do
   echo $x
   x=`expr $x + 1`
done
```

Let's test the program:

```
$ chmod +x until_01.sh
$ ./until_01.sh
```

The following will be the output after executing the preceding commands:

```
0
1
2
3
4
5
6
7
8
9
```

In the following `until_02.sh` script, we ask the user to input text. We are printing text entered on the screen. When the user enters the text quit, the `until` loop ends the iterations:

```
#!/bin/bash
INPUT=""
until [ "$INPUT" = quit ]
do
    echo ""
    echo 'Enter a word (quit to exit) : '
    read INPUT
    echo "You typed : $INPUT"
done
```

Let's test the program:

```
$ chmod +x until_02.sh
$ ./until_02.sh
```

The following will be the output after executing the preceding commands:

```
Enter a word (quit to exit) :
Ganesh
You typed : Ganesh
Enter a word (quit to exit) :
Naik
You typed : Naik
Enter a word (quit to exit) :
quit
You typed : quit
```

In the following `until_03.sh` script, we are passing the username as a the command-line parameter to the script. When required, the user logs in the `grep` command, and they will find it from the output of the `who` command. Then, the `until` loop will stop iterations and provide information on screen about the user login:

```
#!/bin/bash
until who | grep "$1" > /dev/null
do
   sleep 60
done
echo -e \a
echo "***** $1 has just logged in *****"
exit 0
```

Let's test the program:

```
$ chmod +x until_03.sh
$ ./until_03.sh User10
```

The following will be the output after executing the preceding commands:

```
"***** User10 has just logged in *****"
```

This message will be displayed when `user10` has logged in to the server.

Piping the output of a loop to a Linux command

If we need to redirect the output of a loop to any other Linux command such as `sort`, we can even redirect the loop output to be stored in the file:

The following is an example of source code `for_14.sh`:

```
#!/bin/bash
for value in 10 5 27 33 14  25
do
      echo  $value
done | sort -n
```

Let's test the program:

```
$ chmod +x for_14.sh
$ ./for_14.sh
```

The following will be the output after executing the preceding commands:

```
5
10
14
25
27
33
```

In the preceding script, the `for` loop iterates through a list of numbers that is unsorted. The numbers are printed in the body of the loop, which are enclosed between the `do` and `done` commands. Once the loop is complete, the output is piped to the `sort` command, which, in, turn performs a numerical sort and prints the result on screen.

Running loops in the background

In certain situations, the script with loops may take a lot of time to complete. In such situations, we may decide to run the script containing loops in the background so that we can continue other activities in the same terminals. The advantage of this will be that the Terminal will be free to give the next commands.

The following `for_15.sh` script is the technique to run a script with loops in the background:

```
#!/bin/bash
for animal in Tiger Lion Cat Dog
do
     echo $animal
     sleep 1
done &
```

Let's test the program:

```
$ chmod +x for_15.sh
$ ./for_15.sh
```

The following will be the output after executing the preceding commands:

```
Tiger
Lion
Cat
Dog
```

In the preceding script, the `for` loop will process the animals `Tiger`, `Lion`, `Cat`, and `Dog` sequentially. The variable animal will be assigned the animal names one after another. In the `for` loop, the commands to be executed are enclosed between `do` and `done`. The ampersand after the done keyword will make the `for` loop run in the background. The script will run in the background till the `for` loop is complete.

The IFS and loops

The shell has one `environment` variable, which is named the **Internal Field Separator (IFS)**. This variable indicates how the words are separated on the command line. The `IFS` variable is, normally or by default, a whitespace (""). The `IFS` variable is used as a word separator (token) for the `for` command. In many documents, IFS can be any one of the white spaces, :, |, :, or any other desired character. This will be useful while using commands such as `read`, `set`, and `for`. If we are going to change the default `IFS`, then it is a good practice to store the original IFS in a variable.

Later on, when we have done our required tasks, then we can assign the original character back to IFS.

In the following `for_16.sh` script, we are using : as the IFS character:

```
#/bin/bash
cities=Delhi:Chennai:Bangaluru:Kolkata
old_ifs="$IFS"          # Saving original value of IFS
IFS=":"
for place in $cities
do
      echo  The name of city is $place
done
```

Let's test the program:

```
$ chmod +x for_16.sh
$ ./for_16.sh
```

The following will be the output after executing the preceding commands:

```
The name of city is Delhi
The name of city is Chennai
The name of city is Bangaluru
The name of city is Kolkata
```

By default, the original inter-field separator is a whitespace. We have saved the original IFS in the `old_ifs` variable. We assigned a colon : and an IFS in the script. Therefore, we can use : as an inter-field separator in our test file or text string.

Summary

In this chapter, you learned about looping in scripts by working with `for`, `while`, and `until` loops. In order to repeat tasks, such as processing lists, you learned about using the `for`, `while` and `dowhile` loop. You also learned how to control loops using the `break` and `continue` statements.

In the next chapter, you will learn about writing new functions and calling them, sharing data between functions, passing parameters to functions, and creating a library of functions.

10
Working with Functions

In the last chapter, you learned about using decision-making in scripts by working with `test`, `if-else`, and `switch case`. We also used select `for` loop with menu. For repeated tasks, such as processing lists, you learned to use the `for` and `while` loops and the `dowhile`. You also learned about how to control loops using the `break` and `continue` statements.

In this chapter, you will learn the following topics:

- Writing a new function and calling
- Sharing data between functions
- Passing parameters to functions
- Creating a library of functions

Understanding functions

We human beings, in our day-to-day lives, are helped by people who have certain knowledge or skills, such as doctors, lawyers, and barbers. This helps our lives to be more organized and comfortable so that we need not learn every skill in this world. We take advantage of skills that have already been acquired by other people. The same thing applies to software development as well. If we use code or scripts that have already been developed, this will save our time and energy.

In real-world scripts, we break down big tasks or scripts into smaller logical tasks. This modularization of scripts helps in the better development and understanding of code. Functions can be called the smaller logical blocks inside the shell script.

The advantages of functions are as follows:

- If the script is very big, then understanding it becomes very difficult. Using functions, we can easily understand complex script through logical blocks or functions.
- When a big and complex script is divided into functions, then it becomes easy to develop and test the script.
- If a certain part of code is repeated again and again in the big script, then using functions to replace repetitive code is very practical, such as checking whether the file or directory is present or not.
- We define functions for specific tasks or activities. Such functions can be called as commands in scripts.

Functions can be defined on a command line or inside scripts. The syntax for defining functions on a command line is as follows:

```
functionName { command_1; command_2; . . . }
```

We could also use this:

```
functionName() { command_1; command_2; . . }
```

In single-line functions, every command should end with a semicolon.

Let's write a very simple function to illustrate the preceding syntax:

```
$ hello() { echo 'Hello world!';}
```

We can use the previously defined function as follows:

```
$ hello
```

This should produce the following output:

```
Hello world!
```

The syntax of the function declaration inside the shell script is as follows:

```
function_name() {
    block of code
}
```

An alternate function syntax is mentioned here:

```
function function_name
{
    block of code
}
```

Functions should be defined at the beginning of a script.

We can add this function in the shell script `function_01.sh` as follows:

```
#!/bin/bash
hello()
{
    echo "Executing function hello"
}
echo "Script has started now"
hello
echo "Script will end"
```

Test the script as follows:

```
$ chmod +x function_01.sh
$ ./function_01.sh
```

This should produce the following output:

```
Script has started now
Executing function hello
Script will end
```

We can modify the preceding script and create `function_02.sh` with some more functionality, shown as follows:

```
#!/bin/bash
function greet()
{ echo "Hello $LOGNAME, today is $(date)"; }
greet
```

Test the script as follows:

```
$ chmod +x function_02.sh
$ ./function_02.sh
```

This should produce the following output:

```
Hello ganesh, today is Sun Jul 5 22:47:23 PDT 2015
```

The system `init` functions are placed in the `/lib/lsb/init-functions` folder in the Linux operating system:

The script `function_03.sh` has a function for listing the present working directory and listing all the files in the current directory, as follows:

```
#!/bin/bash
function_lister ()
{
    echo "Your present working directory is `pwd`"
    echo "Your files are:"
    ls
}
function_lister
```

Test the script as follows:

```
$ chmod +x function_03.sh
$ ./function_03.sh
```

This should produce the following output:

```
Your present working directory is /home/student/Desktop/test
Your files are:
01.sh  02.sh  03.sh
```

The script `function_04.sh` with a function to pause the script until users press any key is as follows:

```
#!/bin/bash
# pause: causes a script to take a break
pause()
{
echo "To continue, hit RETURN."
read q
}
pause
```

Test the script as follows:

```
$ chmod +x function_04.sh
$ ./function_04.sh
```

Output:

```
To continue, hit  RETURN.
(after hitting any key it resumes)
```

The script `function_05.sh` with a function to print the previous day is as follows:

```
#!/bin/bash
yesterday()
{
date --date='1 day ago'
}
yesterday
```

Test the script as follows:

```
$ chmod +x function_05.sh
$ ./function_05.sh
```

This should produce the following output:

```
Sat Jul  4 22:52:24 PDT 2015
```

The function to convert lowercase letters into uppercase letters is shown in `function_06.sh` as follows:

```
#!/bin/bash
function convert_upper()
{
echo $1 | tr 'abcdefghijklmnopqrstuvwxyz'
               'ABCDEFGHIJKLMNOPQRSTUVWXYZ'
}
convert_upper "ganesh naik - embedded android and linux training"
```

Test the script as follows:

```
$ chmod +x function_06.sh
$ ./function_06.sh
```

This should produce the following output:

```
GANESH NAIK - EMBEDDED ANDROID AND LINUX TRAINING
```

Displaying functions

If you want to see all the declared functions in the shell environment, then enter the following command:

```
$ declare -f
```

If you want to see a particular function, then here is the command:

```
$ declare -f hello
```

This should produce the following output:

```
hello ()
{
    echo 'Hello world!'
}
```

Removing functions

If we no longer need the function in the shell, then we use the following command:

```
$ unset -f hello
$ declare -f hello          # Check the function in shell environment.
```

Nothing will be displayed on the screen, as the `hello` function is removed from the shell environment with the `unset` command.

Passing arguments or parameters to functions

In certain situations, we may need to pass arguments or parameters to functions. In such situations, we can pass arguments as follows.

Calling the script with command-line parameters is as follows:

```
$ name arg1 arg2 arg3 . . .
```

Let's type a function as follows:

```
$  hello() { echo "Hello $1, let us be a friend."; }
```

Call the function in the command line as follows:

```
$ hello Ganesh
```

This should produce the following output:

```
Hello Ganesh, let us be a friend
```

Let's write the script `function_07.sh`. In this script, we pass command-line parameters to the script as well as the function:

```
#!/bin/bash
quit()
{
        exit
}
ex()
{
    echo $1 $2 $3
}
ex Hello hai bye     # Function ex with three arguments
ex World             # Function ex with one argument
echo $1          # First argument passed to script
echo $2          # Second argument passed to script
echo $3          # Third argument passed to script
quit
echo foo
```

Test the script as follows:

```
$ chmod +x function_07.sh
$ ./function_07.sh One Two Three
```

This should produce the following output:

```
Hello hi bye
World
One
Two
Three
```

We can observe from the output that the parameters passed to the function are local to the function. In global scope, the command-line parameters to the script are available as $1, $2, $3, and more.

Another example script, called `function_08.sh`, to pass multiple arguments to the function is as follows:

```
#!/bin/bash
countries()
{
# let us store first argument $1 in variable temp
temp=$1
echo "countries(): $0 = $0"   # print command
echo "countries(): $1 = $1"   # print first argument
```

```
echo "countries(): total number of args passed = $#"
echo "countries(): all arguments ($*) passed = -"$*""
}

# Call function with one argument
echo "Calling countries() for first time"
countries USA

# Call function with three arguments
echo "Calling countries() second time "
countries USA India Japan
```

Test the script as follows:

```
$ chmod +x function_08.sh
$ ./function_08.sh
```

This should produce the following output:

```
Calling countries() for first time
countries(): $0 = ./hello.sh
countries(): $1 = USA
countries(): total number of args passed = 1
countries(): all arguments ($*) passed = -"USA"
Calling countries() second time
countries(): $0 = ./hello.sh
countries(): $1 = USA
countries(): total number of args passed = 3
countries(): all arguments ($*) passed = -"USA India Japan"
```

We can create a function that could create a new directory and change to it during the execution of the program. The script function_09.sh is as follows:

```
#!/bin/bash
# mcd: mkdir + cd; creates a new directory and
# changes into that new directory
mcd ()
{
    mkdir $1
    cd $1
}
mcd test1
```

The preceding script will create the test1 folder in the current folder and change the path to the test1 folder.

A common task in many scripts is to ask users to input an answer as either Yes or No. In such situations, the following script, `function_10.sh` would be very useful:

```
#!/bin/bash
yesno ( )
{
    while  true
    do
    echo "$*"
    echo "Please answer by entering yes or no : "
    read reply
    case $reply in
        yes)
                echo "You answered Yes"
                return 0
                ;;
        no)
                echo "You answered No"
                return 1
                ;;
        * )
                echo "Invalid input"
                ;;
                esac
                done
        }
    yesno
```

Test the script as follows:

```
$ chmod +x function_10.sh
$ ./function_10.sh
```

This should produce the following output:

```
Please answer by entering yes or no:
yes
"You answered Yes"
$ ./function_10.sh
Please answer by entering yes or no:
no
"You answered No"
```

Sharing the data with many functions

We can create variables that may contain strings or numerical values. These global variables can be accessed by all the functions inside a script.

A simple script called `function_11.sh` with functions is as follows:

```
#!/bin/bash
# We will define variable temp for sharing data with function
temp="/temp/filename"

remove_file()
{
  echo "removing file $temp..."
}
remove_file
```

Test the script as follows:

```
$ chmod +x function_11.sh
$ ./function_11.sh
```

This should produce the following output:

```
removing file /temp/filename...
```

Declaring local variables in functions

Whenever we declare a variable in a script, it is accessible to all functions. The variable is global by default. If the variable is modified by any line of script or any function, it will be modified in global scope. This may create problems in certain situations. We will see this problem in the following script, `function_12.sh`:

```
#!/bin/bash
name="John"
hello()
{
   name="Maya"
        echo $name
}
echo $name            # name contains John
hello            # name contains Maya
echo $name            # name contains Maya
```

Test the script as follows:

```
$ chmod +x function_12.sh
$ ./function_12.sh
```

This should produce the following output:

```
John
Maya
Maya
```

To make a variable local, we declare it as follows:

```
local var=value
local varName
```

Let's write the script function_13.sh as follows:

```
#!/bin/bash
name="John"
hello()
{
    local name="Mary"
    echo $name
}
echo $name            # name contains John
hello            # name contains Mary
echo $name            # name contains John
```

Test the script as follows:

```
$ chmod +x function_13.sh
$ ./function_13.sh
```

Output:

```
John
Mary
John
```

The `local` command can only be used within a function. The `local` keyword limits the scope of the variable to the function. In the previous script, we initially declared the `name` variable; it has global scope. This `name` variable has the content `John`. Then, we have declared the `local` variable `name` in the `hello` function. This local variable `name` is initialized to `Mary`. Then, outside of the `hello` function, we again access the global variable `name`, which has the content `John`.

Returning information from functions

You have learned to pass command-line parameters to functions. Similarly, the function can return integers as a return value. Normally, functions return either *TRUE* or *FALSE*. In certain cases, the function can return integer values, such as `5` or `10`, as well.

The syntax is:

```
return N
```

When the function calls the command return, the function exits with the value specified by N.

If the function does not call the command return, then the exit status returned is that of the last command executed in the function. If what we need is the status of the last command executed in the function, then we need not return any value from the function. This is illustrated in the following script, `function_14.sh`:

```
#!/bin/bash
is_user_root() { [ $(id -u) -eq 0 ]; }
is_user_root && echo "You are root user, you can go ahead."
|| echo "You need to be administrator to run this script"
```

Test the script as follows:

```
$ chmod +x function_14.sh
$ ./function_14.sh
```

If you are a root user, then the output will be as follows:

```
You are root user, you can go ahead.
```

If you are a normal user, then the output will be as follows:

```
You need to be administrator to run this script
```

A modified version of the previous script is `function_15.sh`:

```
#!/bin/bash
declare -r TRUE=0
declare -r FALSE=1

is_user_root()
{
[ $(id -u) -eq 0 ] && return $TRUE || return $FALSE
}
is_user_root && echo "You can continue" || echo "You need to be root to run
this script."
```

Test the script as follows:

```
$ chmod +x function_15.sh
$ ./function_15.sh
```

This should produce the following output:

You need to be root to run this script.

Let's see the script in which the function returns a value:

```
#!/bin/bash
yes_or_no()
{
echo "Is your name $*?"
while true
do
echo -n "Please reply yes or no :"
read reply
case $reply in
Y | y | yes ) return 0;;
N | n | no ) return 1;;
*) echo "Invalid answer"
esac
done
}

if yes_or_no $1
then
echo"Hello $1 "
else
echo"name not provided"
fi
```

Test the script as follows:

```
$ chmod +x function_16.sh
$ ./function_16.sh Ganesh
```

This should produce the following output:

```
Is your name Ganesh?
Please reply yes or no : yes
Hello Ganesh
```

Returning a word or string from a function

In shell scripts, functions cannot return a word or string from a function. If we need to pass data to a script then we will have to store it in a global variable. We can even use echo or print to send data to a pipe or redirect it to the log file.

Running functions in the background

We have already seen in previous chapters that to run any command in the background, we have to terminate the command using &:

```
$ command &
```

Similarly, we can make the function run in the background by appending & after the function call. This will make the function run in the background so that the Terminal will be free:

```
#!/bin/bash
dobackup()
{
    echo "Started backup"
    tar -zcvf /dev/st0 /home >/dev/null 2>& 1
    echo "Completed backup"
}
dobackup &
echo -n "Task...done."
echo
```

Test the script as follows:

```
$ chmod +x function_17.sh
$ ./function_17.sh
```

This should produce the following output:

```
Task...done.
Started backup
Completed backup
```

Command source and period (.)

Normally, whenever we enter a command, the new process gets created. If we want to make functions from the script to be made available in the current shell, then we need a technique that will run the script in the current shell instead of creating a new shell environment. The solution to this problem is using either the source or . commands.

The commands, source and ., can be used to run the shell script in the current shell instead of creating a new process. This helps with declaring functions and variables in the current shell.

The syntax is as follows:

```
$ source filename [arguments]
```

Or you can use the following:

```
$ . filename [arguments]
$ source functions.sh
```

Or you could use this:

```
$ . functions.sh
```

If we pass command-line arguments, these will be handled inside a script as $1, $2, and more:

```
$ source functions.sh arg1 arg2
```

Or you could enter the following:

```
$ ./path/to/functions.sh arg1 arg2
```

The source command does not create a new shell. It runs the shell scripts in the current shell so that all the variables and functions will be available in the current shell for usage.

Creating a library of functions

If we want to create our own library of functions, then we can create a script and add all the functions into this script. We can make all the functions from our script `functions.sh` available in the current shell by calling `source` or the period `.` command.

The procedure to load all functions into the current shell is as follows:

```
$ country USA
```

Since the `country` function is not a part of the shell environment, this command will give an error:

```
$ . functions.sh
```

Or it could display this one:

```
$ source functions.sh
$ country USA India Japan
```

This will execute the `country` function along with the parameter, `USA India Japan`.

We can even load a script containing library functions inside another script as follows:

```
#!/bin/bash
. /../my-libray.sh
call_library_functions();
```

We have called the library function script `my-library.sh` inside another script. This will define all the functions within the script `my-library.sh` available in the current script environment.

Summary

In this chapter, you learned about the functions in shell scripts. You also learned about defining and displaying functions and removing the functions from a shell. In addition to this, you learned about passing arguments to functions, sharing data between functions, declaring local variables in functions, returning results from functions, and running functions in the background. And, finally, you learned about using the `source` and `.` (dot) commands. We used these commands to use the library of functions.

In the next chapter, you will learn about using `traps` and `signals`. You will also learn about creating menus with the help of the `dialog` utility.

11
Using Advanced Functionality in Scripts

In the last chapter, you learned about using functions in shell scripts and defining, displaying, and removing functions from the shell. You also learned about passing arguments to functions, sharing data between functions, declaring local variables in functions, returning results from functions, and running functions in the background. At the end, you learned about using `source` and `.` commands. You used these commands for using a library of functions.

In this chapter, you will learn the following topics:

- Understanding signals and traps
- Graphical menu development using the `dialog` utility

Understanding signals and traps

Two types of interrupts exist in the Linux operating system: hardware interrupts and software interrupts. Software interrupts are called signals or traps. Software interrupts are used for inter-process synchronizations.

Signals are used to notify us about a certain event occurrence or to initiate a certain activity.

We use software signals many times. For example, if any command does not respond after being typed, then you might have entered *Ctrl + C*. This sends a `SIGINT` signal to the process, and the process is terminated. In certain situations, we may want the program to perform a certain activity instead of terminating it using *Ctrl + C*. In such cases, we can use the `trap` command to ignore a signal or to associate our desired function with that signal.

In operating systems, software interrupts or signals are generated when the process attempts to divide a number by zero or sometimes due to power failure, system hang up, illegal instruction execution, or invalid memory access.

The action, performed by a few signals, terminates the process. We can configure the shell to make the following responses:

- Catch the signal and execute user-defined programs
- Ignore the signal
- Suspend the process (similar to *Ctrl + Z*)
- Continue the process, which was suspended earlier

Enter either of the following commands to get the full list of all signals:

```
$ kill -l
$ trap -l
```

Output:

```
[student@localhost work]$ kill -l
 1) SIGHUP       2) SIGINT       3) SIGQUIT      4) SIGILL       5) SIGTRAP
 6) SIGABRT      7) SIGBUS       8) SIGFPE       9) SIGKILL     10) SIGUSR1
11) SIGSEGV     12) SIGUSR2     13) SIGPIPE     14) SIGALRM     15) SIGTERM
16) SIGSTKFLT   17) SIGCHLD     18) SIGCONT     19) SIGSTOP     20) SIGTSTP
21) SIGTTIN     22) SIGTTOU     23) SIGURG      24) SIGXCPU     25) SIGXFSZ
26) SIGVTALRM   27) SIGPROF     28) SIGWINCH    29) SIGIO       30) SIGPWR
31) SIGSYS      34) SIGRTMIN    35) SIGRTMIN+1  36) SIGRTMIN+2  37) SIGRTMIN+3
38) SIGRTMIN+4  39) SIGRTMIN+5  40) SIGRTMIN+6  41) SIGRTMIN+7  42) SIGRTMIN+8
43) SIGRTMIN+9  44) SIGRTMIN+10 45) SIGRTMIN+11 46) SIGRTMIN+12 47) SIGRTMIN+13
48) SIGRTMIN+14 49) SIGRTMIN+15 50) SIGRTMAX-14 51) SIGRTMAX-13 52) SIGRTMAX-12
53) SIGRTMAX-11 54) SIGRTMAX-10 55) SIGRTMAX-9  56) SIGRTMAX-8  57) SIGRTMAX-7
58) SIGRTMAX-6  59) SIGRTMAX-5  60) SIGRTMAX-4  61) SIGRTMAX-3  62) SIGRTMAX-2
63) SIGRTMAX-1  64) SIGRTMAX
```

If we want to know which keys are used for particular signals, then we enter the following command:

```
$ stty -a
```

The following is a list of a few of the standard signals that a process can use:

Number	Name	Description	Action
0	EXIT	The shell exits.	Termination
1	SIGHUP	The terminal has been disconnected.	Termination
2	SIGINT	The user presses *Ctrl + C*.	Termination

Number	Name	Description	Action
3	SIGQUIT	The user presses *Ctrl + \\.*	Termination
4	SIGILL	This gives an illegal hardware instruction.	Program error
5	SIGTRAP	This is produced by the debugger.	Program error
8	SIGFPE	This gives an arithmetical error, such as division by zero.	Program error
9	SIGKILL	This cannot be caught or ignored.	Termination

We can send either of the kill signals to a process with PID # 1234 as follows:

```
kill -9 1234
kill -KILL 1234
kill -SIGKILL 1234
```

As we can see, we can use a signal number or a signal name along with the process ID. By default, the kill command sends signal number 15 to the process. Using the kill command, we can send the desired signal to any specific process.

We can suspend a process using the *Ctrl + Z* signal as follows:

```
$ kill -19 pid
```

Ctrl + Z or SIGTSTP will suspend the process.

We can restart the suspended process by sending the SIGCONT signal.

```
$ kill -18 pid
```

The signal number of SIGCONT is 18.

Using the trap command

If a signal or software interrupt is generated while the script is running, then we can define what action is performed by that interrupt handler using the trap command. The trap command helps us in re-assigning the system response to a particular signal through the user-defined function or commands.

The syntax to use the `trap` command is either of the following:

```
$ trap 'command; command' signal-name
$ trap 'command; command' signal-number
```

The usage as per the preceding syntax is as follows:

```
trap 'echo "You pressed Control key" '  0 1 2 15
```

This will print the message `You pressed Control key`, when any of the signals `SIGINT`, `SIGHUP`, or `SIGTERM` are received by the process:

```
trap 'rm file.tmp; echo "file.tmp is deleted" ' INT TERM HUP
```

When any of the `SIGINT`, `SIGTERM`, or `SIGHUP` signals arrive, then they will delete the `file.tmp` file and print the message.

While using the `trap` command, if the command string is surrounded by double quotes, then the command substitution and variable substitution will be done during the `trap` command execution. If the command `string` is enclosed in single quotes then the command substitution and variable substitution will be done when the signal is detected.

Ignoring signals

If we want the shell to ignore certain signals, then we can call the `trap` command followed by a pair of empty quotes as a command. Those signals will be ignored by the shell process shown by either of the following commands:

```
$ trap " " 2 3 20
$ trap " " INT QUIT TSTP
```

The signals `2 (SIGINT)`, `3 (SIGQUIT)`, and `20 (SIGTSTP)` will be ignored by the shell process.

Resetting signals

If we want to reset the signal behavior to the original default action, then we need to call the `trap` command followed by the signal name or number as shown in the following examples, respectively:

```
$ trap TSTP
$ trap 20
```

This will reset the default action of signal 20 (SIGTSTP). The default action is to suspend the process (*Ctrl + Z*).

Listing traps

Let's reassign our function to signals with the trap command:

```
$ trap 'echo "You pressed Control key" '  0 1 2 15
```

If we do not pass any arguments after the trap command, then it lists all reassigned signals along with their functions.

We can list all the assigned signal lists with the following command:

```
$ trap
```

Output:

```
trap -- 'echo "You pressed Control key" ' EXIT
trap -- 'echo "You pressed Control key" ' SIGHUP
trap -- 'echo "You pressed Control key" ' SIGINT
trap -- 'echo "You pressed Control key" ' SIGTERM
```

Using traps inside a function

If we use the trap command inside a function in the script, then the reassigned signal behavior will become global inside a script. We can check this effect in the following script example.

Let's write shell script trap_01.sh as follows:

```
#!/bin/bash
trap "echo  caught signal SIGINT" SIGINT
trap "echo  caught signal SIGQUIT" 3
trap "echo  caught signal SIGTERM" 15
while :
do
    sleep 50
done
```

Let's test the program as follows:

```
$ chmod +x trap_01.sh
$ ./trap_01.sh
```

Output:

```
^Ccaught signal SIGINT
^Quit (core dumped)
caught signal SIGQUIT
```

Let's write one more trap_02.sh shell script as follows:

```
#!/bin/bash

trap "echo  caught signal SIGINT" SIGINT
trap "echo  caught signal SIGQUIT" 3
trap "echo  caught signal SIGTERM" 15
trap "echo  caught signal SIGTSTP" TSTP

echo "Enter any string (type 'bye' to exit)."
while true
do
    echo "Rolling...c"
    read string
    if [ "$string" = "bye" ]
    then
        break
    fi
done
echo "Exiting normally"
```

Let's test the program as follows:

```
$ chmod +x trap_02.sh
$ ./trap_02.sh
```

Output:

```
Enter any string (type 'bye' to exit).
Rolling...c
^Ccaught signal SIGINT
bye
Exiting normally
```

Running scripts or processes even if the user logs out

Sometimes, we may need our script to run even after we log out, such as when making a backup and similar activities. In this case, even if we log out, the system is powered on and running. In such situations, we can use the nohup command. The nohup command prevents the process from terminating by using the SIGHUP signal.

The nohup command makes our script run without attaching it to a Terminal. Therefore, if we use the echo command to print text on the Terminal it will not be printed in a Terminal, since the script is not attached to a Terminal. In such cases, we need to redirect the output to the file, or nohup will automatically redirect the output to a nohup.out file.

Therefore, if we need to run a process, even if we log out, we need to use the nohup command as follows:

```
$ nohup command &
```

The example is as follows:

```
$ nohup sort emp.lst &
```

This will run a program to sort the emp.lst file in the background.

```
$ nohup date &
```

Creating dialog boxes with the dialog utility

The dialog utility is used to create a basic-level graphical user interface. We can use this in shell script to create very useful programs.

To install the dialog utility in Debian or Ubuntu Linux, enter the following command:

```
$ sudo apt-get update
$ sudo apt-get install 1 dialog
```

Similarly, enter the following command to install the utility dialog in CentOS or Red Hat Linux:

```
$ sudo yum install dialog
```

The typical syntax of the `dialog` command is as follows:

```
$ dialog --common-options --boxType "Text" Height Width
                                    --box-specific-option
```

The `common-options` utility is used to set the background color, title, and so on in dialog boxes.

The option details are as follows:

- `Text`: The caption or contents of the box
- `Height`: The height of the dialog box
- `Width`: The width of the dialog box

Creating a message box (msgbox)

To create a simple message box, we can use the following command:

```
$ dialog --msgbox "This is a message." 10 50
```

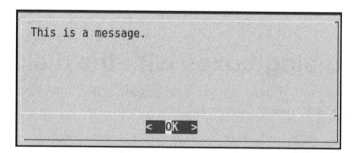

Creating a message box (msgbox) with a title

Enter the following command to create a message box with the following title:

```
$ dialog --title "Hello" --msgbox 'Hello world!' 6 20
```

The option details are as follows:

- --title "Hello": This will set the title of the message box to "Hello"
- --msgbox 'Hello world!': This will set the content of the message box to "Hello world!"
- 6: This will set the height of the message box
- 20: This will set the width of message box:

The message box has a **Hello** title with content **Hello World**! It has a single **OK** button. We can use this message box to inform the user about any events or information. The user will have to press *Enter* to close this message box. If the content is large for a message box, then the dialog utility will provide the scrolling of the message.

The yes/no box (yesno)

If we need to obtain a yes or no answer from the user, we can use the following options along with the dialog command:

```
$ dialog --yesno "Would you like to continue?" 10 50
```

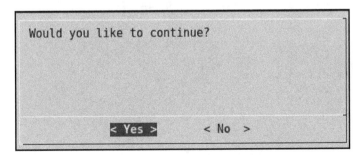

We can have the same yes/no dialog box with a title as follows:

```
$ dialog --title "yesno box" --yesno "Would you like to continue?" 10
50
```

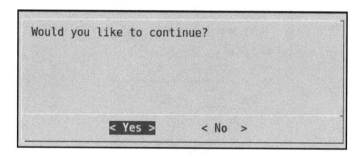

Let's write the dialog_01.sh shell script as follows:

```
#!/bin/bash
dialog --title "Delete file"
--backtitle "Learning Dialog Yes-No box"
--yesno "Do you want to delete file "~/work/sample.txt"?" 7 60

# Selecting "Yes" button will return 0.
# Selecting "No" button will return 1.
# Selecting [Esc] will return 255.
result=$?
case $result in
    0)      rm ~/work/sample.txt
     echo "File deleted.";;
    1)      echo "File could not be deleted.";;
    255)    echo "Action Cancelled - Presssed [ESC] key.";;
esac
```

Let's test the following program:

```
$ chmod +x dialog_01.sh
$ ./dialog_01.sh
```

Output:

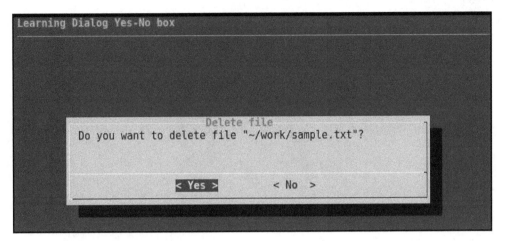

The input box (inputbox)

Whenever we want to ask a user to input text via the keyboard, in such situations, the `inputbox` option is useful. While entering text via the keyboard, we can use keys such as Delete, Backspace, and the arrow cursor keys for editing. If the input text is larger than the input box, the input field will be scrolled. Once the **OK** button is pressed, the input text can be redirected to a text file:

```
# dialog  --inputbox  "Please enter something."  10  50
2> /tmp/tempfile
VAR=`cat ~/work/output.txt
```

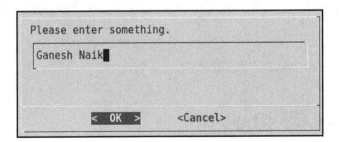

Let's write the `dialog_02.sh` shell script to create an input box as follows:

```
#!/bin/bash
result="output.txt"
```

```
>$ $result     # Create empty file
dialog --title "Inputbox Demo"
--backtitle "Learn Shell Scripting"
--inputbox "Please enter your name " 8 60 2>$result

response=$?
name=$(<$result)
case $response in
0)    echo "Hello $name"
      ;;
1)    echo "Cancelled."
      ;;
255)     echo "Escape key pressed."
esac
rm $result
```

Let's test the following program:

```
$ chmod +x dialog_02.sh
$ ./dialog_02.sh
```

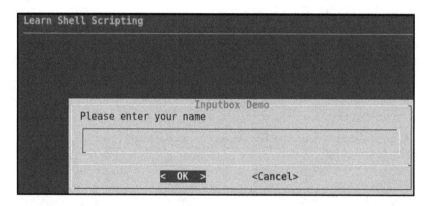

Output:

"Hello Ganesh Naik"

The textbox (textbox)

If we want to display the contents of the file in a textbox inside the menu created by a dialog, then enter the following command:

```
$ dialog  --textbox /etc/passwd 10  50
```

```
root:x:0:0:root:/root:/bin/bash
bin:x:1:1:bin:/bin:/sbin/nologin
daemon:x:2:2:daemon:/sbin:/sbin/nologin
adm:x:3:4:adm:/var/adm:/sbin/nologin
lp:x:4:7:lp:/var/spool/lpd:/sbin/nologin
sync:x:5:0:sync:/sbin:/bin/sync
                                                    6%
                    < EXIT >
```

We are displaying the /etc/passwd file in the textbox with the previous command.

A password box

Many times, we need a password from the user. In this case, the password should not be visible on the screen. The password box option is perfect for this purpose.

If we want to display an entered password as a string of ****, then we will need to add the --insecure option.

We will need to redirect the inserted password to a file.

Let's write dialog_03.sh shell script to receive the password as follows:

```
#!/bin/bash
# creating the file to store password
result="output.txt 2>/dev/null"

# delete the password stored file, if program is exited pre-maturely.
trap "rm -f output.txt" 2 15

dialog --title "Password"
--insecure
--clear
--passwordbox "Please enter password" 10 30 2> $result

reply=$?

case $reply in
   0)    echo "You have entered Password :  $(cat $result)";;
   1)    echo "You have pressed Cancel";;
   255)   cat $data && [ -s $data ] || echo "Escape key is pressed.";;
esac
```

Let's test the following program:

```
$ chmod +x dialog_03.sh
$ ./dialog_03.sh
```

Output:

```
You have entered Password :   adcd1234
```

The checklist box (checklist)

In this case, we can present the user with a choice to select one or multiple options from a list:

```
# dialog --checklist "This is a checklist" 10 50 2
"a" "This is one option" "off"
"b" "This is the second option" "on"
```

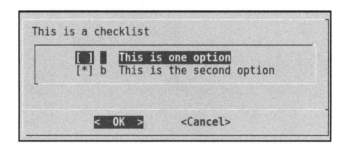

The menu box (menu)

Usually, a program or shell script may be required to perform multiple types of tasks. In such cases, the menu box option is very useful. This option will display a list of choices for the user. Then, the user may select an option of their own choice. Our script should execute the desired option.

Each menu has two fields, a tag and an item string. In the next example menu demo, we have tags such as date, calendar, and editor. A description of a tag is called an item string.

Let's write the `dialog_04.sh` shell script to create a menu as follows:

```bash
#!/bin/bash
# Declare file to store selected menu option
RESPONSE=menu.txt
# Declare file to store content to display date and cal output
TEMP_DATA=output.txt
vi_editor=vi
# trap and delete temp files
trap "rm $TEMP_DATA; rm $RESPONSE; exit" SIGHUP SIGINT SIGTERM

function display_output(){
    dialog --backtitle "Learning Shell Scripting" --title "Output" --clear
--msgbox "$(<$TEMP_DATA)" 10 41
}

function display_date(){
    echo "Today is `date` @ $(hostname -f)." >$TEMP_DATA
    display_output 6 60 "Date and Time"
}

function display_calendar(){
    cal >$TEMP_DATA
    display_output 13 25 "Calendar"
}

# We are calling infinite loop here
while true
do

# Show main menu
dialog --help-button --clear --backtitle "Learn Shell Scripting"
--title "[ Demo Menubox ]"
--menu "Please use up/down arrow keys, number keysn
1,2,3.., or the first character of choicen
as hot key to select an option" 15 50 4
Calendar "Show the Calendar"
Date/time "Show date and time"
Editor "Start vi editor"
Exit "Terminate the Script" 2>"${RESPONSE}"

menuitem=$(<"${RESPONSE}")

# Start activity as per selected choice
case $menuitem in
    Calendar) display_calendar;;
    Date/time) display_date;;
```

```
    Editor) $vi_editor;;
    Exit) echo "Thank you !"; break;;
esac
done
# Delete temporary files
[ -f $TEMP_DATA ] && rm $TEMP_DATA
[ -f $RESPONSE ] && rm $RESPONSE
```

Let's test the following program:

```
$ chmod +x dialog_04.sh
$ ./dialog_04.sh
```

Output:

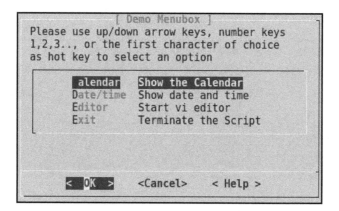

The radiolist box (radiolist)

If you want the user to select only one option out of many choices, then `radiolist` is a suitable option:

```
# dialog --radiolist  "This is a selective list, where only one
option can be chosen" 10 50 2
"a" "This is the first option" "off"
"b" "This is the second option" "on"
```

Radio buttons are not square but round, as can be seen in the following screenshot:

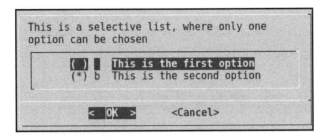

The progress meter box (gauge)

The progress meter displays a meter at the bottom of the box. This meter indicates the percentage of the process completed. New percentages are read from standard input, one integer per line. This meter is updated to reflect each new percentage.

Let's write the dialog_05.sh shell script to create a progress meter as follows:

```
#!/bin/bash
declare -i COUNTER=1
{
    while test $COUNTER -le 100
        do
            echo $COUNTER
            COUNTER=COUNTER+1
            sleep 1
    done
} | dialog --gauge  "This is a progress bar"  10 50 0
```

Let's test the following program:

```
$ chmod +x dialog_05.sh
$ ./dialog_05.sh
```

Output:

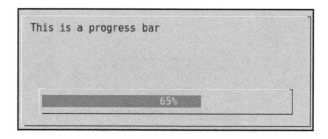

Customization of dialog with the configuration file.

We can customize dialog using the ~/.dialogrc configuration file. The default file location is $HOME/.dialogrc.

To create the .dialogrc configuration file, enter the following command:

```
$ dialog --create-rc ~/.dialogrc
```

We can customize the output of the dialog utility by changing any of the configuration parameters defined in the .dialogrc file.

Summary

In this chapter, you learned about using traps and signals. You also learned about creating menus with the help of the dialog utility.

In the next chapter, you will learn about Linux system startup, from power-on to login/logout of the user, and how to customize a Linux system environment.

12
System Startup and Customizing a Linux System

In the last chapter, you learned about using traps and signals. You also learned about creating menus with the help of the dialog utility.

In this chapter, you will learn about Linux system startup, from power-on to user login, and how to customize a Linux system environment.

System startup, inittab, and run levels

When we power on the Linux system, shell scripts are run one after another and the Linux system is initialized. These scripts start various services, daemons, databases, and applications, as well as mount discs. Even during the shutting down of the system, certain shell scripts are executed so that important system data and information can be saved to the disk and the applications are properly shut down. These are called boot, startup, and shutdown scripts. These scripts are copied during installation of the Linux operating system in your computer. As a developer or administrator, understanding these scripts may help you in understanding and debugging the Linux system. If required, you can customize these scripts if the need arises.

The kernel startup and init process

In our computers, there is one EPROM chip called the **BIOS**, which is situated on the motherboard or main board of our computers. When we power-on, the processor starts executing a program from the BIOS. The program in the BIOS does a power-on-self-test, checking memory and other peripherals. Then the BIOS program initializes the basic hardware required for PC operation, such as initializing the PCI bus, video devices, and similar.

Finally, the BIOS checks the boot device sequence and queries the first boot device. This BIOS program then reads the master boot record of the first boot device, which is normally a hard disk, USB device, or DVD. Once the BIOS reads the master boot record of the first boot device, then the boot loader is started. The boot loader reads the kernel binary and copies it to the RAM memory. The boot loader checks if the kernel binary is clean and not corrupt. If the integrity check is good then it uncompresses the kernel in the RAM. The bootloader then calls the start_kernel() function, which is a part of kernel source code. Once the start_kernel() function is called, the kernel is started.

The kernel then initializes its subsystems, such as process management, filesystem, device drivers, memory management, network management, and similar other modules of the kernel. Then, it mounts the root file system, and the kernel creates the first process called init. This init process reads the /etc/inittab file. In inittab, the run level information is stored. As per this information, the operating system is initialized by the init process.

The typical /etc/inittab content will be as follows:

```
$ cat /etc/inittab
```

Here is the output:

```
# inittab is no longer used when using systemd.
#
# ADDING CONFIGURATION HERE WILL HAVE NO EFFECT ON YOUR SYSTEM.
#
# Ctrl-Alt-Delete is handled by /usr/lib/systemd/system/ctrl-alt-
del.target
#
# systemd uses 'targets' instead of runlevels. By default, there are
two main targets:
#
# multi-user.target: analogous to runlevel 3
# graphical.target: analogous to runlevel 5
#
# To view current default target, run:
# systemctl get-default
#
# To set a default target, run:
# systemctl set-default TARGET.target
#
```

In the preceding line, the number 5 after ID specifies that the system should be started in run level 5. It means that the system should be started in X11, such as a graphical user interface. We will study more about run levels in the next section.

Nowadays, various Linux distributions, including CentOS, have replaced the init process with the systemd daemon program, which initializes Linux by starting processes and services in parallel instead of serial execution.

The process ID of the systemd process is always 1, since it is the first process created by the kernel.

systemd reads the file linked by /etc/systemd/system/default.target to determine the default system target. The default system target is equivalent to the run level. Then, as per the desired run level, system initialization is continued.

Understanding run levels

There are seven run levels. The system will be started in run level 1 to 5. Run level 0 is used for shutting down the system. Run level 6 is used for rebooting the system. The graphical user interface is started in run level 5. The following is the summary of the different run levels:

Sr. No.	Run level number	Description
1	0	Halting the system
2	1	Single-user mode
3	2	Multi-user mode
4	3	Multi-user with network support
5	4	Not used
6	5	Graphical user interface with multi-user and networking support
7	6	Rebooting the system

We need to be in the root-user mode to use the init command.

If we give the following command, then the system will shut down:

```
# init 0
```

To reboot the system, use the following command:

```
# init 6
```

If the system is running in the command-line mode, and you want to start your server in the graphical user mode, then use the following command:

```
# init 5
```

System initialization boot scripts

In the Linux system, the following folders will be present in the /etc/ folder:

Sr. No.	Folder name	Description
1	rc0.d/	The scripts called during shutting down
2	rc1.d/	The run level 1 scripts
3	rc2.d/	The run level 2 scripts
4	rc3.d/	The run level 3 scripts
5	rc4.d/	The run level 4 scripts
6	rc5.d/	The run level 5 scripts
7	rc6.d/	The run level 6 scripts
8	rcS.d/	The scripts called during boot-up, before every run level
9	rc.local	The final script called after run level initialization

Every run level folder will have script names starting with either S or K. When starting the system, the scripts with names starting with S are called one after another. When shutting down, all the script names starting with K are called one after another.

For example, if the system has to be started in run level 5, then initially all the scripts from the rcS.d folder will be called, then all the scripts from rc5.d will be called. Finally, the rc.local script will be called.

The content of /etc/rc.local is as follows:

```
$ cat /etc/rc.local
```

Here is the output:

```
#!/bin/bash
# THIS FILE IS ADDED FOR COMPATIBILITY PURPOSES
#
# It is highly advisable to create own systemd services or udev rules
# to run scripts during boot instead of using this file.
#
# In contrast to previous versions due to parallel execution during
boot
# this script will NOT be run after all other services.
#
# Please note that you must run 'chmod +x /etc/rc.d/rc.local' to ensure
# that this script will be executed during boot.
touch /var/lock/subsys/local
exit 0
```

We can add our customization commands before the exit 0 line in the preceding rc.local script.

Before any user is logged in, the previously mentioned scripts will be called. After this, user login initialization will be started. This is explained in the following sections.

User initialization scripts

So far, we have seen different scripts that initialize the operating system prior to a user login. Once the basic operating system is initialized, the user login process starts. This process is explained in the following topics.

System-wide setting scripts

In the /etc/ folder, the following files are related to the user level initialization:

- /etc/profile: A few distributions will have an additional folder called /etc/profile.d/. All the scripts from the profile.d folder will be executed.
- /etc/bash.bashrc.

The preceding scripts are called by every user, including root and normal users. Initially, the /etc/profile script will be called. This script initializes system-wide environment settings. A few distributions will have the /etc/profile.d/ folder. SUSE Linux has an additional /etc/profile.local script. The scripts in this folder will also be called. Then, the /etc/bash.bashrc script will be executed.

User level settings – default files

Scripts in the /etc/ folder will be called for all users. Particular, user-specific initialization scripts are located in the HOME folder of each user. These are as follows:

- $HOME/.bash_profile: This contains user-specific bash environment default settings. This script is called during the login process.
- $HOME/.bash_login: This contains the second user environment initialization script called during the login process.
- $HOME/.profile: If present, this script internally calls the .bashrc script file.
- $HOME/.bashrc: This is an interactive shell or terminal initialization script.

All the preceding script names start with a dot. These are hidden files. We will need to give the ls -a command to view these files.

- Non-login shells

Whenever we create a new shell Terminal, such as when we press the *Ctrl + Alt + T* key combination, or we start a Terminal from the applications tab, then the Terminal that is created is called the interactive shell Terminal. We use this Terminal to interact with the operating system. This is not the login shell, which is created during the boot-up process, but this is an interactive shell Terminal that gives us the CLI prompt for entering the commands to execute.

Whenever we create an interactive Bash Terminal, shell scripts from /etc/profile and similar are not called, only the ~/.bashrc script is called. This happens every time we create a new interactive shell terminal. If we want environment customization for every newly created interactive shell Terminal, we need to customize the .bashrc script from the home folder of the user.

If you check the content of $HOME/.bashrc, you will observe the following:

- The .bashrc script is setting the prompt
- It initializes the environmental variables, HISTCONTROL, HISTSIZE, and HISTFILESIZE
- It customizes the output of the less command
- It creates various alias commands such as grep, fgrep, egrep, ll, la, l, and similar

If we customize .bashrc, such as adding new alias commands or declaring a new function or environment variables, then we should execute .bashrc for it to take effect. The following are two ways to run the .bashrc script so that the environment of the current shell will also be updated as per the customization done in the .bashrc script:

```
$ source .bashrc
$ . .bashrc
```

Please note the usage of .(dot) two occasions, the first time for the command .(dot) and the second time in the script name, which we want to call.

With these two techniques, the child shell is not created but the .bashrc script runs in the current shell environment. Therefore, all updated or newly created environment variables become part of the current shell environment.

Every user's home folder has one more script called .bash_logout. This script is called or executed when the user exits from the login shell.

If the system user is an embedded system developer, and is interested in adding or modifying the device's driver-related commands, then they will have to make changes in the /etc/rc*.d folder scripts, or they may have to modify the /etc/rc.local script.

If the administrator wants to modify the environment for all users, then they will have to modify the /etc/profile and /etc/bash_bashrc scripts.

If we want to customize the environment related to a particular user, then the scripts located in the user's home folder, such as $HOME/.profile, $HOME/bash_profile, and $HOME/bash_login scripts, should be modified.

If the user wants to customize only the interactive shell Terminal environment, then they will have to customize the $HOME/.bashrc script.

If you are working in system administration, then I would suggest you learn about the /etc/fstab file and its editing. This file is used for configuring mount points and how file systems are mounted.

Summary

In this chapter, you learned about Linux system startup, from power-on to user login, and how to customize a Linux system environment.

In the next chapter, you will learn about using stream editor (sed) and awk for text processing.

13
Pattern Matching and Regular Expressions with sed and awk

In the previous chapter, you learned about a Linux system's startup process, from power-on to user login, and how to customize a Linux system environment.

In this chapter, we will cover the following topics:

- Understanding regular expressions
- Stream editor (sed) for text processing
- Using awk for text processing

The basics of regular expressions

A sequence of characters that have certain patterns of text (with meta-characters) that are searched for in a larger text file are called **regular expressions**:

```
$ ll /proc | grep cpuinfo
```

In the preceding command, the grep utility will search for the cpuinfo text in all lines of input text and will print lines that have the cpuinfo text.

Utilities such as `grep`, `sed`, and `awk` use regular expressions for filtering text and then apply various processing commands as required by the user. The lines that do not match the pattern will be rejected. The following diagram explains the same concept:

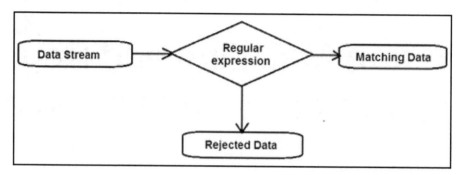

In `Chapter 3`, *Using Test Processing and Filters in Your Scripts*, you learned about the basics of regular expressions and pattern matching using the vi editor and the `grep` utility.

sed – non-interactive stream editor

The stream editor (`sed`) is a very popular non-interactive stream editor. Normally, whenever we edit files using the vi editor, we need to open the file using the `vi` command, then we interact with the file to see the content of the file on screen, then edit it, and then save the file. Using `sed`, we can type commands on the command line and `sed` will make the changes to the text file. `sed` is a non-destructive editor. `sed` makes the changes to the file and displays the content on screen. If we want to save the changed file, then we need to redirect the output of `sed` to the file.

The procedure to install `sed` is shown here.

For Ubuntu or any Debian-based distributions, enter the following command:

```
$ apt-get install sed
```

For Red Hat or any rpm-based distribution enter the following command:

```
$ yum install sed
```

To check the version of `sed`, enter the following command:

```
$ sed -V
```

Otherwise, enter this command:

```
$ sed --version
GNU sed version 3.02
```

Understanding sed

Whenever you use `sed` commands on a text file, `sed` reads the first line of the file and stores it in a temporary buffer called **pattern space**. `sed` processes this pattern space buffer as per commands given by the user. Then, it prints the output on screen. This line from the pattern space is then removed and the next line of the file is loaded in the pattern space. In this way, it processes all the lines one by one. This line-by-line processing is continued till the last line of the file. As the `sed` commands are processed in the temporary buffer or pattern space, the original line is not modified. Therefore, we say `sed` is a non-destructive buffer:

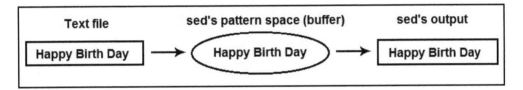

Understanding regular expression usage in sed

While using `sed`, regular expressions are enclosed in forward slashes, as `grep` and `sed` use regular expressions and meta-characters for searching patterns in the file. An example of this would be the following:

```
sed -n '/Regular_Expression/p' filename
sed -n '/Mango/p' filename
```

This will print lines matching the `Mango` pattern:

```
sed -n 's/RE/replacement string/' filename
sed -n 's/Mango/Apple/p' filename
```

This will find the line containing the `Mango` pattern and then the `Mango` pattern will be replaced by the `Apple` text. This modified line will be shown on screen and the original file will be unchanged.

The following is a summary of various meta-characters and their usage in sed:

Meta-character Function

^	This is the beginning-of-line anchor
$	This is the end-of-line anchor
.	This matches one character, but not the newline character
*	This matches zero or more characters
[ ]	This matches one character in the set
[^]	This matches one character not in the set
(..)	This saves matched characters
&	This saves the search string so it can be remembered in the replacement string
<	This is the beginning-of-word anchor
>	This is the end-of-word anchor
x{m}	This is the repetition of the character x:m times
x{m,}	This means at least m times
x{m,n}	This means between m and n times

Addressing in sed

We can specify which line or number of lines the pattern search and commands are to be applied on while using the sed commands. If line numbers are not specified, then the pattern search and commands will be applied to all lines of the input file.

The line numbers on which commands are to be applied are called the **address**. The address can be a single line number or range of lines in which the starting number of the line and the ending number of the range will be separated by commas. Ranges can be composed of numbers, regular expressions, or a combination of both.

The sed commands specify actions such as printing, removing, replacing, and so on.

The syntax is as follows:

```
sed 'command' filename(s)
```

Here is an example:

```
$ cat myfile | sed '1,3d'
```

You could also use the following:

```
sed '1,3d' myfile
```

This will delete lines 1 to 3:

```
sed -n '/[Aa]pple/p' item.list
```

If the Apple or apple pattern is found in the item.list file, then those lines will be printed on screen and the original myfile file will be unchanged.

To negate the command, the exclamation character (!) can be used.

Here's an example:

```
sed '/Apple/d' item.list
```

This tells sed to delete all the lines containing the Apple pattern.

Consider the following example:

```
sed '/Apple/!d' item.list
```

This will delete all the lines except the line containing the Apple pattern.

How to modify a file with sed

sed is a non-destructive editor. This means the output of sed is displayed on screen but the original file is unchanged. If we want to modify the file, then we can redirect the output of the sed command to the file. Deleting lines is illustrated in the following examples:

```
$ sed '1,3d' datafile > tempfile
$ mv tempfile newfile
```

In this example, we have deleted lines 1 to 3 and stored the output in tempfile. Then, we have to rename tempfile to newfile.

Printing – the p command

By default, the action of the `sed` command is to print the pattern space, such as every line that is copied into the buffer, and then print the result of processing it. Therefore, the `sed` output will consist of all lines along with the processed line by sed. If we do not want the default pattern space line to be printed, then we need to give the −n option. Therefore, we should use the −n option and the p command together to see the result of the `sed` processed output.

Here is an example:

```
$ cat country.txt
```

The output is as follows:

```
Country     Capital      ISD Code
USA         Washington   1
China       Beijing      86
Japan       Tokyo        81
India       Delhi        91
$ sed '/USA/p' country.txt
```

The output is as follows:

```
Country     Capital      ISD Code
USA         Washington   1
USA         Washington   1
China       Beijing      86
Japan       Tokyo        81
India       Delhi        91
```

All the lines from the file are printed by default and the lines with the USA pattern are also printed:

```
$ sed -n '/USA/p' country.txt
```

The output is as follows:

```
USA   Washington   1
```

As we have given the −n option, `sed` has suppressed default printing of all lines from the country file but has printed the line that contains the text pattern USA.

Deleting – the d command

The d command is used to delete lines. After sed copies a line from a file and puts it into a pattern buffer, it processes commands on that line, and, finally, displays the contents of the pattern buffer on screen. When the d command is issued, the line currently in the pattern buffer is removed and not displayed, as follows:

```
$ cat country.txt
Country       Capital       ISD Code
USA           Washington    1
China         Beijing       86
Japan         Tokyo         81
India         Delhi         91
$ sed '3d' country.txt
```

The output is as follows:

```
Country       Capital       ISD Code
USA           Washington 1
Japan         Tokyo               81
India         Delhi         91
```

Here is the explanation.

The output will contain all the lines except the third line. The third line is deleted by the following command:

```
$ sed '3,$d' country.txt
```

The output is as follows:

```
Country       Capital    ISD Code
USA           Washington       1
```

This will delete the third line to the last line. The dollar sign in the address indicates the last line. The comma is called a **range operator**:

```
$ sed '$d' country.txt
```

The output is as follows:

```
Country       Capital    ISD Code
USA           Washington       1
China         Beijing          86
Japan         Tokyo            81
```

Here is the explanation.

This deletes the last line. All lines except lines will be displayed.

Here is an example:

```
$ sed '/Japan/d' country.txt
```

The output is as follows:

```
Country      Capital          ISD Code
USA          Washington    1
China        Beijing          86
India        Delhi            91
```

The line containing the `Japan` pattern is deleted. All other lines are printed:

```
$ sed '/Japan/!d' country.txt
```

The output is as follows:

```
Japan        Tokyo            81
```

This has deleted all the lines that do not contain `Japan`.

Let's see a few more examples with the `delete` command.

This will delete line 4 and the next five lines:

```
$ sed '4,+5d'
```

This will keep lines 1 to 5 and delete all the other lines:

```
$ sed '1,5!d'
```

This will delete lines 1, 4, 7, and so on:

```
$ sed '1~3d'
```

Starting from 1, every third line step increments. The number that follows the tilde is what is called the **step increment**. The step increment indicates the following:

```
$ sed '2~2d'
```

This will delete every other line, starting with line 2.

Substitution – the s command

If we want to substitute some text with new text, then we can use commands. After the forward slash, the regular expression is enclosed and then the text to be substituted is placed. If the g option is used, then substitution will happen globally, meaning that it will be applied to the full document. Otherwise, only the first instance will be substituted:

```
$ cat shopping.txt
```

The output is as follows:

```
Product      Quantity    Unit_Price   Total_Cost
Apple        2           3            6
Orange            2           .8           1.6
Papaya            2           1.5          3
Chicken      3           5            15
Cashew            1           10           10
$ sed 's/Cashew/Almonds/g' shopping.txt
```

The output is as follows:

```
Product      Quantity    Unit_Price   Total_Cost
Apple        2           3            6
Orange            2           .8           1.6
Papaya            2           1.5          3
Chicken      3           5            15
Almonds      1           10           10
```

The s command has replaced Cashew with Almonds. The g flag at the end indicates that the substitution is to be applied globally. Otherwise, it will be applied to the first pattern match only.

The following substitution command will replace two-digit numbers at the end of the line with .5 appended to them:

```
$ sed 's/[0-9][0-9]$/&.5/' shopping.txt
```

The output is as follows:

```
Product      Quantity    Unit_Price   Total_Cost
Apple        2           3            6
Orange            2           .8           1.6
Papaya            2           1.5          3
Chicken           3           5            15.5
Cashew            1           10           10.5
```

The ampersand in the search pattern represents the exact pattern found. This will be replaced by the exact pattern with `.5` appended to it.

Range of selected lines the comma

To use `sed` effectively, we should be clear about how to define range. **Range** is typically two addresses in a file as follows:

- Range with numbers:

```
'6d': range of line 6
'3,6d': range from line 3 to 6
```

- Range with pattern:

```
'/pattern1/,/pattern2/
```

- This will specify the range of all the lines between `pattern1` and `pattern2`. We can even specify the range with a combination of both, that is, `'/pattern/,6'`. This will specify the range of lines between the pattern and line `6`.

As mentioned, we can specify the range as numbers, pattern, or a combination of both, as shown here.

```
$ cat country.txt
Country      Capital          ISD Code
USA          Washington   1
China        Beijing          86
Japan        Tokyo            81
India        Delhi            91
$ sed -n '/USA/,/Japan/p' country.txt
```

The output is as follows:

```
USA      Washington    1
China    Beijing       86
Japan    Tokyo         81
```

In this example, all the lines between addresses starting with USA and until the pattern Japan will be printed on screen, as shown here.

```
$ sed -n '2,/India/p' country.txt
```

The output is as follows:

```
USA         Washington    1
China       Beijing            86
Japan       Tokyo         81
India       Delhi              91
```

In this example, line 2 to the pattern India, are printed on screen as shown here.

```
$ sed '/Apple/,/Papaya/s/$/**   Out of Stock   **/' shopping.txt
```

The output is as follows:

```
Product         Quantity Unit_Price  Total_Cost
Apple       2          3             6**       Out of Stock    **
Orange           2          .8          1.6**     Out of Stock
**
Papaya           2         1.5          3**       Out of Stock
**
Chicken          3         5           15
Cashew           1        10           10
```

In this example, for all the lines between the Apple and Papaya patterns, the end of line will be replaced by the ** Out of Stock ** string.

Multiple edits – the e command

If we need to perform multiple editing with the same command, then we can use the -e command. Each edit command should be separated by the -e command. sed will apply each editing command separated by -e on the pattern space before loading the next line in the pattern space:

```
$ cat shopping.txt
```

The output is as follows:

```
Product         Quantity Unit_Price  Total_Cost
Apple       2          3             6
Orange           2          .8            1.6
Papaya      2         1.5           3
Chicken     3         5            15
Cashew           1        10           10
```

This is an example:

```
sed -e '5d' -e 's/Cashew/Almonds/' shopping.txt
```

The output is as follows:

Product	Quantity	Unit_Price	Total_Cost
Apple	2	3	6
Orange	2	.8	1.6
Papaya	2	1.5	3
Almonds	1	10	10

Initially, the command for deleting the fifth line is called, then, the next substitution command to replace Cashew with Almonds is processed.

Reading from files – the r command

If we need to insert text from another file into a file, processed by sed, then we can use the r command. We can insert text from another file to the specified location:

Here is an example:

```
$ cat new.txt
```

The output will be:

```
********************************
    Apples are out of stock
********************************
$ sed '/Apple/r new.txt' shopping.txt
```

The output is as follows:

Product	Quantity	Unit_Price	Total_Cost
Apple	2	3	6

```
********************************
    Apples are out of stock
********************************
```

Orange	2	.8	1.6
Papaya	2	1.5	3
Chicken	3	5	15
Cashew	1	10	10

This command has added the content of the new.txt file after the line containing the Apple pattern.

Writing to files – the w command

The `sed` command for writing is `w`. Using this command, we can write lines from one file to another file.

Here is an example:

```
$ cat new.txt
```

The output is as follows:

```
new is a empty file
$ sed -n '/Chicken/w new.txt' shopping.txt
$ cat new.txt
Chicken     3     5     15
```

After the `w` command, we specify the file to which we will perform the write operation. In this example, the line containing the `Chicken` pattern is written to the `new.txt` file.

Appending – the a command

The `a` command is used for **appending**. When the append command is used, it appends the text after the line in the pattern space in which the pattern is matched. The backslash should be placed immediately after the `a` command. On the next line, the text to be appended is to be placed.

Here is an example:

```
$ cat shopping.txt
```

The output is as follows:

```
Product      Quantity   Unit_Price   Total_Cost
Apple        2          3            6
Orange       2           .8          1.6
Papaya       2          1.5          3
Chicken      3          5            15
Cashew       1          10           10
$ sed '/Orange/a
**** Buy one get one free offer on this item ! ****' shopping.txt
```

The output is as follows:

```
Product     Quantity  Unit_Price  Total_Cost
Apple       2         3           6
Orange      2           .8        1.6
**** Buy one get one free offer on this item ! ****
Papaya      2           1.5       3
Chicken     3           5         15
Cashew      1           10        10
```

The new text **** Buy one get one free offer on this item ! **** is appended after the line containing the Orange pattern.

Inserting – the i command

The i command is used for **inserting** text above the current pattern space line. When we use the append command, new text is inserted after the current line, which is in the pattern buffer. In this similar-to-append command, the backslash is inserted after the i command.

Here is an example:

```
$ cat shopping.txt
Product     Quantity  Unit_Price  Total_Cost
Apple       2         3           6
Orange             2           .8            1.6
Papaya             2           1.5           3
Chicken     3           5           15
Cashew      1           10          10
$ sed '/Apple/i
        New Prices will apply from Next month ! ' shopping.txt
```

The output is as follows:

```
Product     Quantity  Unit_Price  Total_Cost
        New Prices will apply from Next month !
Apple       2         3           6
Orange      2           .8        1.6
Papaya      2           1.5       3
Chicken     3           5         15
Cashew      1           10        10
```

In this example, the new text, New Prices will be applied from next month! is inserted before the line containing the Apple pattern. Please check the i command and the backslash following it.

Changing – the c command

The c command is the **change** command. It allows sed to modify or change existing text with new text. The old text is overwritten with the new:

```
$ cat shopping.txt
```

The output is as follows:

```
Product       Quantity   Unit_Price   Total_Cost
Apple         2          3            6
Orange        2           .8          1.6
Papaya        2          1.5          3
Chicken       3          5            15
Cashew        1          10           10
```

Here is an example:

```
$ sed '/Papaya/c
    Papaya is out of stock today !' shopping.txt
```

The output is as follows:

```
Product   Quantity   Unit_Price   Total_Cost
Apple     2          3            6
Orange    2           .8          1.6
   Papaya is out of stock today !
Chicken   3          5            15
Cashew    1          10           10
```

In this example, the line containing the expression `Papaya` is changed to the new line, `Papaya is out of stock today!`.

Transform – the y command

The **transform** command is similar to the Linux `tr` command. The characters are translated according to the character sequence given. For example, `y/ABC/abc/` will convert lowercase `abc` into uppercase `ABC`.

Here is an example:

```
$ cat shopping.txt
```

The output will be:

```
Product       Quantity  Unit_Price  Total_Cost
Apple         2         3           6
Orange        2          .8         1.6
Papaya        2         1.5         3
Chicken       3         5           15
Cashew        1         10          10
$ sed '2,4y/abcdefghijklmnopqrstuvwxyz/ABCDEFGHIJKLMNOPQRS
TUVWXYZ/' shopping.txt
```

The output will be:

```
Product   Quantity  Unit_Price  Total_Cost
APPLE     2         3           6
ORANGE    2          .8         1.6
PAPAYA    2         1.5         3
Chicken   3         5           15
Cashew    1         10          10
```

In this example, for lines 2, 3, and 4, all the lowercase letters are converted to uppercase letters.

Quit – the q command

The q command is used for **quitting** the sed processing without proceeding to the next line:

```
$ cat shopping.txt
```

The output will be as follows:

```
Product       Quantity  Unit_Price  Total_Cost
Apple         2         3           6
Orange        2          .8         1.6
Papaya        2         1.5         3
Chicken       3         5           15
Cashew        1         10          10
```

Here is an example:

```
$ sed '3q' shopping.txt
```

The output will be as follows:

```
Product   Quantity   Unit_Price   Total_Cost
Apple     2          3            6
Orange    2           .8          1.6
```

In this example, after printing the first to third lines, sed quits further processing.

Holding and getting – the h and g commands

We have already seen that sed has a pattern buffer. sed has one more type of buffer called a **holding buffer**. With the h command, we can inform sed to store the pattern buffer in the holding buffer. Whenever we need the line that is stored in the pattern buffer, we can get it with the g command, that is, get the buffer.

Here is an example:

```
$ sed -e '/Product/h' -e '$g' shopping.txt
```

The output is as follows:

```
Product   Quantity   Unit_Price   Total_Cost
Apple     2          3            6
Orange    2           .8          1.6
Papaya    2          1.5          3
Chicken   3          5            15
Cashew    1          10           10
Product   Quantity   Unit_Price   Total_Cost
```

In this example, the line containing the Product pattern is stored in the holding buffer by the h command. Then, the next editing command asks sed to get the line from the holding buffer when the last line of the file is reached. It then appends the line from the holding buffer after the last line of the file.

Holding and exchanging – the h and x commands

This is an **exchange** command. By using this command, we can exchange the holding buffer with the current line in the pattern buffer.

Here is an example:

```
$ sed -e '/Apple/h'  -e '/Cashew/x' shopping.txt
```

The output is as follows:

```
Product   Quantity   Unit_Price   Total_Cost
Apple     2          3            6
Orange    2          .8           1.6
Papaya    2          1.5          3
Chicken   3          5            15
Apple     2          3            6
```

In this example, the line with the `Apple` pattern is stored in the holding buffer. When the pattern with `Cashew` is found, that line will be exchanged with the holding buffer.

sed scripting

The `sed` script file contains a list of `sed` commands in a file. To inform `sed` about our script file, we should use the `-f` option before the script filename. If the `sed` commands are not separated by a new line, then every command should be separated by a colon `":"`. We should make sure that there aren't any trailing whitespaces after any of the commands in the `sed` script file; otherwise, `sed` will give an error. `sed` takes each line in the pattern buffer and then it will process all commands on that line. After this line is processed, the next line will be loaded in the pattern buffer. For the continuation of any `sed` command that cannot be fitted on one line, we need to add one backslash at the end of the line to inform it of the continuation.

Here is an example:

```
$ cat shopping1.txt
```

The output is as follows:

```
Product    Quantity   Unit_Price
Apple      200        3
Orange     200        .8
Papaya     100        1.5
Chicken    65         5
Cashew     50         10
April, third week
$ cat stock
```

The output is as follows:

```
# This is my first sed script by :
1i
Stock status report
/Orange/a
Fresh Oranges are not available in this season.
Fresh Oranges will be available from next month
/Chicken/c
*********************************************************
We will not be stocking this item for next few weeks.
*********************************************************
$d
```

Enter the following command:

```
$ sed -f stock shopping1.txt
```

The output is as follows:

```
Stock status report
Product    Quantity  Unit_Price
Apple      200         3
Orange     200          .8
Fresh Oranges are not available in this season.
Fresh Oranges will be available from next month
Papaya     100         1.5
*********************************************************
We will not be stocking this item for next few weeks.
*********************************************************
Cashew     50     10
```

In this script, the following processing has taken place:

1. The comment line starts with the pound (#) sign.
2. The command 1i informs sed to insert the next text before line number 1.
3. The command /Orange/a informs sed to append the next text after the line containing the Orange pattern.
4. The command /Chicken/c informs sed to replace the line containing the Chicken pattern by the next line.
5. The last command, $d, tells sed to delete the last line of the input file.

Using awk

awk is a program that has its own programming language for performing data-processing and generating reports.

The GNU version of awk is gawk.

awk processes data, which can be received from a standard input, input file, or as the output of any other command or process.

awk processes data similar to sed, line by line. It processes every line for the specified pattern and performs specified actions. If the pattern is specified, then all the lines containing specified patterns will be displayed. If pattern is not specified, then the specified actions will be performed on all the lines.

The meaning of awk

The name of the program awk is made from the initials of the three authors of the language, namely Alfred **A**ho, Peter **W**einberger, and Brian **K**ernighan. It is not very clear why they selected the name awk instead of kaw or wak!

Using awk

The following are different ways to use awk:

- Syntax while using only pattern:

```
$ awk 'pattern' filename
```

- In this case, all the lines containing pattern will be printed.

- Syntax using only action:

```
$ awk '{action}' filename
```

- In this case, action will be applied to all lines.

- Syntax using pattern and action:

```
$ awk 'pattern {action}' filename
```

- In this case, action will be applied on all the lines containing pattern.

As seen previously, the `awk` instruction consists of patterns, actions, or a combination of both.

Actions will be enclosed in curly brackets. Actions can contain many statements separated by a semicolon or a newline.

`awk` commands can be on the command line or in the `awk` script file. The input lines could be received from a keyboard, pipe, or file.

Input from files

Let's see a few examples of using the preceding syntax using input from files:

```
$ cat people.txt
```

The output is as follows:

```
Bill Thomas   8000   08/9/1968
Fred Martin   6500   22/7/1982
Julie Moore   4500   25/2/1978
Marie Jones   6000   05/8/1972
Tom Walker    7000   14/1/1977
```

Enter the following command:

```
$ awk '/Martin/' people.txt
```

The output is as follows:

```
Fred Martin   6500   22/7/1982
```

This prints a line containing the `Martin` pattern.

Here is an example:

```
$ cat people.txt
```

The output is as follows:

```
Bill Thomas   8000   08/9/1968
Fred Martin   6500   22/7/1982
Julie Moore   4500   25/2/1978
Marie Jones   6000   05/8/1972
Tom Walker    7000   14/1/1977
```

Enter the following command:

```
$ awk '{print $1}' people.txt
```

The output is as follows:

```
Bill
Fred
Julie
Marie
Tom
```

This awk command prints the first field of all the lines from the people.txt file:

```
$ cat people.txt
```

The output is as follows:

```
Bill Thomas   8000   08/9/1968
Fred Martin   6500   22/7/1982
Julie Moore   4500   25/2/1978
Marie Jones   6000   05/8/1972
Tom Walker    7000   14/1/1977
```

Here is an example:

```
$ awk '/Martin/{print $1, $2}' people.txt
Fred Martin
```

This prints the first and second field of the line that contains the Martin pattern.

Input from commands

We can use the output of any other Linux command as an input to the awk program. We need to use the pipe to send an output of another command as the input to the awk program.

The syntax is as follows:

```
$ command | awk 'pattern'
$ command | awk '{action}'
$ command | awk 'pattern {action}'
```

Here is an example:

```
$ cat people.txt | awk '$3 > 6500'
```

The output is as follows:

```
Bill Thomas   8000   08/9/1968
Tom Walker    7000   14/1/1977
```

This prints all lines where field 3 is greater than 6500.

Here is an example:

```
$ cat people.txt | awk '/1972$/{print $1, $2}'
```

The output is as follows:

```
Marie Jones
```

This prints fields 1 and 2 of the lines that ends with the 1972 pattern:

```
$ cat people.txt | awk '$3 > 6500 {print $1, $2}'
```

This prints fields 1 and 2 of the lines where the third field is greater than 6500.

How awk works

Let's understand how the awk program processes every line. We will consider a simple file, sample.txt:

```
$ cat sample.txt
Happy Birth Day
We should live every day.
```

Let's consider the following awk command:

```
$ awk '{print $1, $3}' sample.txt
```

The following diagram shows how awk will process every line in memory:

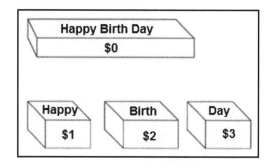

An explanation of the preceding diagram is as follows:

- awk reads a line from the file and puts it into an internal variable called $0. Each line is called a record. By default, every line is terminated by a new line.
- Then, every record or line is divided into separate words or fields. Every word is stored in numbered variables $1, $2, and so on. There can be as many as 100 fields per record.
- awk has an internal variable called **internal field separator (IFS)**. IFS is normally whitespace. Whitespace includes tabs and spaces. The fields will be separated by IFS. If we want to specify any other IFS, such as colon (:) in the /etc/passwd file, then we will need to specify it in the awk command line.

When awk checks an action as '{print $1, $3}', it tells awk to print the first and third fields. Fields will be separated by a space. The command is as follows:

```
$ awk '{print $1, $3}' sample.txt
```

The output will be as follows:

```
Happy Day
We live
```

An explanation of the output is as follows:

- There is one more internal variable called **Output Field Separator (OFS)**. This is normally space. This will be used for separating fields while printing as output.
- Once the first line is processed, awk loads the next line in $0 and it continues as discussed earlier.

awk commands from within a file

We can put awk commands in a file. We will need to use the -f option before using the awk script filename to use the awk script file for all processing instructions. awk will copy the first line from the data file to be processed in $0, and then it will apply all processing instructions on that record. Then, it will discard that record and load the next line from the data file. This way, it will proceed till the last line of the data file. If the action is not specified, the pattern-matching lines will be printed on screen. If the pattern is not specified, then the specified action will be performed on all lines of the data file.

This is an example:

```
$ cat people.txt
Bill Thomas   8000   08/9/1968
Fred Martin   6500   22/7/1982
Julie Moore   4500   25/2/1978
Marie Jones   6000   05/8/1972
Tom Walker    7000   14/1/1977
$ cat awk_script
/Martin/{print $1, $2}
```

Enter the following command:

```
$ awk -f awk_script people.txt
```

The output is as follows:

```
Fred Martin
```

The awk command file contains the Martin pattern and it specifies the action of printing fields 1 and 2 of the line, matching the pattern. Therefore, it has printed the first and second fields of the line containing the Martin pattern.

Records and fields

Every line terminated by the new line is called a **record** and every word separated by a whitespace is called a **field**. We will learn more about them in this section.

Records

awk does not see the file as one continuous stream of data; it processes the file line by line. Each line is terminated by a newline character. It copies each line in an internal buffer, called a record.

The record separator

By default, a new line or carriage return is an input record separator and output record separator. The input record separator is stored in the built-in variable RS, and the output record separator is stored in ORS. We can modify the ORS and RS, if required.

The $0 variable

The entire line that is copied into the buffer, such as a record, is called $0.

Take the following command, for example:

```
$ cat people.txt
```

The output is will be as follows:

```
Bill Thomas   8000   08/9/1968
Fred Martin   6500   22/7/1982
Julie Moore   4500   25/2/1978
Marie Jones   6000   05/8/1972
Tom Walker    7000   14/1/1977
$ awk '{print $0}' people.txt
```

The output is as follows:

```
Bill Thomas   8000   08/9/1968
Fred Martin   6500   22/7/1982
Julie Moore   4500   25/2/1978
Marie Jones   6000   05/8/1972
Tom Walker    7000   14/1/1977
```

This has printed all the lines of the text file. Similar results can be seen with the following command:

```
$ awk '{print}' people.txt
```

The NR variable

awk has a built-in variable called **NR**. It stores the record number. Initially, the value stored in NR is 1. Then, it will be incremented by one for each new record.

Take, for example, the following command:

```
$ cat people.txt
```

The output will be:

```
Bill Thomas   8000   08/9/1968
Fred Martin   6500   22/7/1982
Julie Moore   4500   25/2/1978
Marie Jones   6000   05/8/1972
Tom Walker    7000   14/1/1977
$ awk '{print NR, $0}' people.txt
The output will be:
1 Bill Thomas   8000   08/9/1968
2 Fred Martin   6500   22/7/1982
3 Julie Moore   4500   25/2/1978
4 Marie Jones   6000   05/8/1972
5 Tom Walker    7000   14/1/1977
```

This has printed every record, such as $0 with a record number, which is stored in NR. That is why we see 1, 2, 3, and so on before every line of output.

Fields

Every line is called a record, and every word in a record is called a **field**. By default, words or fields are separated by whitespace, that is, *Space* or *Tab*. awk has an internal built-in variable called NF, which will keep track of field numbers. Typically, the maximum field number will be 100 and will depend on implementation. The following example has five records and four fields.

```
$1      $2        $3        $4
Bill Thomas   8000   08/9/1968
Fred Martin   6500   22/7/1982
Julie Moore   4500   25/2/1978
Marie Jones   6000   05/8/1972
Tom Walker    7000   14/1/1977
$ awk '{print NR, $1, $2, $4}' people.txt
```

The output will be:

```
1 Bill Thomas 08/9/1968
2 Fred Martin 22/7/1982
3 Julie Moore 25/2/1978
4 Marie Jones 05/8/1972
5 Tom Walker  14/1/1977
```

This has printed the record number and field numbers 1, 2, and so on, on the screen.

Field separators

Every word is separated by whitespace. We will learn more about them in this section.

The input field separator

We have already discussed that an input field separator is a whitespace by default. We can change this IFS to other values on the command line or by using the BEGIN statement. We need to use the -F option to change the IFS.

This is an example:

```
$ cat people.txt
```

The output will be as follows:

```
Bill Thomas:8000:08/9/1968
Fred Martin:6500:22/7/1982
Julie Moore:4500:25/2/1978
Marie Jones:6000:05/8/1972
Tom Walker:7000:14/1/1977
$ awk -F: '/Marie/{print $1, $2}' people.txt
```

The output will be as follows:

```
Marie Jones 6000
```

We have used the -F option to specify colon (:) as IFS instead of the default, IFS. Therefore, it has printed field 1 and 2 of the records in which the Marie pattern was matched. We can even specify more than one IFS on the command line as follows:

```
$ awk -F'[ :t]' '{print $1, $2, $3}' people.txt
```

This will use *Space, colon,* and *Tab* characters as the inter field separator or IFS.

Patterns and actions

While executing commands using `awk`, we need to define patterns and actions. Let's learn more about them in this section.

Patterns

`awk` uses patterns to control the processing of actions. When a pattern or regular expression is found in the record, an action is performed, or if no action is defined then `awk` simply prints the line on the screen.

This is an example:

```
$ cat people.txt
```

The output will be:

```
Bill Thomas   8000   08/9/1968
Fred Martin   6500   22/7/1982
Julie Moore   4500   25/2/1978
Marie Jones   6000   05/8/1972
Tom Walker    7000   14/1/1977
$ awk '/Bill/' people.txt
```

The output will be:

```
Bill Thomas   8000   08/9/1968
```

In this example, when the `Bill` pattern is found in the record, that record is printed on screen:

```
$ awk '$3 > 5000' people.txt
```

The output will be:

```
Bill Thomas   8000   08/9/1968
Fred Martin   6500   22/7/1982
Marie Jones   6000   05/8/1972
Tom Walker    7000   14/1/1977
```

In this example, when field `3` is greater than `5000`, that record is printed on the screen.

Actions

Actions are performed when the required pattern is found in a record. Actions are enclosed in curly brackets ({ and }). We can specify different commands in the same curly brackets, but those should be separated by a semicolon.

The syntax is as follows:

```
pattern{ action statement; action statement; .. }
      or
pattern
{    action statement
        action statement
}
```

The following example gives a better idea:

```
$ awk '/Bill/{print $1, $2 ", Happy Birth Day !"}' people.txt
```

This is the output:

```
Bill Thomas, Happy Birth Day !
```

Whenever a record contains the Bill pattern, awk performs the action of printing field 1, field 2, and prints the message Happy Birth Day.

Regular expressions

A regular expression is a pattern enclosed in forward slashes. A regular expression can contain meta-characters. If the pattern matches any string in the record, then the condition is true and any associated action, if mentioned, will be executed. If no action is specified, then the record is simply printed on the screen.

Meta-characters used in awk regular expressions are as follows:

Meta-character	What it does
.	A single character is matched
*	Zero or more characters are matched
^	The beginning of the string is matched
$	The end of the string is matched
+	One or more of the characters are matched
?	Zero or one of the characters are matched

`[ABC]`	Any one character in the set of characters A, B, or C is matched
`[^ABC]`	Any one character not in the set of characters A, B, or C is matched
`[A-Z]`	Any one character in the range from A to Z is matched
`a|b`	Either a or b is matched
`(AB)+`	One or more sets of (AB); such as AB, ABAB, and so on is matched
`*`	A literal asterisk is matched
`&`	This is used to represent the replacement string when it is found in the search string

In the following example, all lines containing the regular expression `Moore` will be searched and the matching record's field 1 and 2 will be displayed on the screen:

```
$ awk  '/Moore/{print $1, $2}' people.txt
```

The output is as follows:

```
Julie Moore
```

Writing the awk script file

Whenever we need to write multiple patterns and actions in a statement, then it is more convenient to write a script file. The script file will contain patterns and actions. If multiple commands are on the same line, then those should be separated by a semicolon; otherwise, we need to write them on separate lines. The comment line will start by using the pound (#) sign.

Here is an example:

```
$ cat people.txt
```

The output is as follows:

```
Bill Thomas   8000   08/9/1968
Fred Martin   6500   22/7/1982
Julie Moore   4500   25/2/1978
Marie Jones   6000   05/8/1972
Tom Walker    7000   14/1/1977
```

(The `awk` script)

```
$ cat report
```

The output is as follows:

```
/Bill/{print "Birth date of " $1, $2 " is " $4}
/^Julie/{print $1, $2 " has a salary of  $" $3 "."}
/Marie/{print NR, $0}
```

Enter the following command:

```
$ awk -f report people.txt
```

The output will be as follows:

```
Birth date of Bill Thomas is 08/9/1968
Julie Moore has a salary of $4500.
4 Marie Jones   6000   05/8/1972
```

In this example, the awk command is followed by the -f option, which specifies the script file as a record and then processes all the commands in the text file, people.txt.

In this script, the regular expression Bill is matched, then we print text, field 1, field 2, and then the birth date information. If the regular expression Julie is matched at the start of the line, then print her salary information. If the regular expression Marie is matched, then print the record number NR and print the complete record.

Using variables in awk

We can simply declare a variable in the awk script, even without any initialization. Variables can be of type string, number, floating type, and so on. There is no type declaration required such as in C programming. awk will find out the type of variable by its right-hand side data type during initialization or its usage in the script.

Uninitialized variables will have the value 0 or strings will have a value null such as " ", depending on how it is used inside scripts:

```
name = "Ganesh"
```

The variable name is of the string type:

```
j++
```

The variable j is a number. Variable j is initialized to zero and it is incremented by one:

```
value = 50
```

The `value` variable is a number with an initial value of `50`.

The technique to modify the string type variable to the number type is as follows:

```
name + 0
```

The technique to modify the number type variable to the string type is as follows:

```
value " "
```

User-defined variables can be made up of letters, digits, and underscores. The variable cannot start with a digit.

Decision-making using an if statement

In awk programming, the `if` statement is used for decision-making. The syntax is as follows:

```
if (conditional-expression)
   action1
else
   action2
```

If the condition is true, then `action1` will be performed, else `action2` will be performed. This is very similar to C programming `if` constructs.

An example of using the `if` statement in the `awk` command is as follows:

```
$ cat person.txt
```

The output is as follows:

```
Bill Thomas    8000    08/9/1968
Fred Martin    6500    22/7/1982
Julie Moore    4500    25/2/1978
Marie Jones    6000    05/8/1972
Tom Walker     7000    14/1/1977
$ awk '{
if ($3 > 7000) { print "person with salary more than 7000 is n", $1, "
" , $2;}
}' people.txt
```

The output is as follows:

```
person with salary more than 7000 is
Bill Thomas
```

In this example, field 3 is checked to see whether it is `greater than 7000` for any record. If field 3 is greater than `7000` for any record, then the action of printing the name of the person and value of the third record will be done.

Using the for loop

The `for` loop is used for doing certain actions repetitively. The syntax is as follows:

```
for(initialization; condition; increment/decrement)
actions
```

Initially, a variable is initialized then the condition is checked. If it is true, then the action or actions enclosed in curly brackets are performed. Then, the variable is incremented or decremented. Again, the condition is checked. If the condition is true, then actions are performed; otherwise, the loop is terminated.

An example of the `awk` command with the `for` loop is as follows:

```
$ awk '{ for( i = 1; i <= NF; i++) print NF,$i }' people.txt
```

Initially, the `i` variable is initialized to 1. Then, the condition is checked to see whether `i` is less than `NF`. If true, then the action of printing `NF` and the field is performed. Then `i` is incremented by one. Again, the condition is checked to see whether it is true or false. If true, then it will perform actions again; otherwise, it will terminate the looping activity.

Using the while loop

Similar to C programming, `awk` has a `while` loop for doing tasks repeatedly. `while` will check for the condition. If the condition is true, then actions will be performed. If a condition is false, then it will terminate the loop.

The syntax is as follows:

```
while(condition)
    actions
```

An example of using the `while` construct in `awk` is as follows:

```
$ cat people.txt
$ awk '{ i  = 1; while ( i <= NF ) { print NF, $i ; i++ } }' people.txt
```

NF is the number of fields in the record. The variable i is initialized to 1. Then, while i is smaller or equal to NF, the print action will be performed. The print command will print fields from the record from the people.txt file. In the action block, i is incremented by one. The while construct will perform the action repeatedly until i is less than or equal to NF.

Using the do while loop

The do while loop is similar to the while loop; but the difference is, even if the condition is true, at least once the action will be performed unlike the while loop.

The syntax is as follows:

```
do
action
while (condition)
```

After the action or actions are performed, the condition is checked again. If the condition is true, then the action will be performed again; otherwise, the loop will be terminated.

The following is an example of using the do while loop:

```
$ cat awk_script
BEGIN {
  do {
     ++x
     print x
  } while ( x <= 4 )
}
$ awk -f awk_script
1
2
3
4
5
```

In this example, x is incremented to 1 and the value of x is printed. Then, the condition is checked to see whether x is less than or equal to 4. If the condition is true, then the action is performed again.

Summary

In this chapter, you learned about regular expressions and about using `sed` and `awk` for text processing. You learned various commands and the usage of options along with a lot of examples for using `sed` and `awk`. In this example, the value of x is set in the body of the loop using the auto-increment operator. The body of the loop is executed once and the expression is evaluated.

14
Taking Backup and Embedding Other Languages in Shell Scripts

In the previous chapter, you learned about regular expressions and using `sed` and `awk` for text processing. You learned various commands and the usage of options, along with a lot of examples for using `sed` and `awk`.

In this chapter, we will cover the following topics:

- Taking backup of local or remote data
- Automating database administration

Backup of files from command line

In IT or our day-to-day computer industry activities, taking backup is one of the most important activities. Previously, offices were required to keep important paper in a safe place; but if a fire breaks out, then everything is finished. In the digital world, taking backup makes our life easier and safeguards us against data loss.

There are many software tools available on the market for taking software backups. We will study one of the most popular software backup command-line utilities, `rsync`.

Backup command rsync

The command-line utility `rsync` is the most widely used backup command in Linux for backing up or synchronizing data. This utility was developed in 1996 by Andrew Tridgell and Paul Mackerras.

This utility is mostly installed in all popular Linux distributions. If it is not installed, then run the following commands:

For CentOS or Red Hat:

```
# yum install rsync
```

For Debian or Ubuntu

```
# apt-get install rsync
```

`rsync` is a powerful utility. It can copy or synchronize files in the same computer or across the network in another continent-based computer over the internet.

The basic syntax for using `rsync` is as follows:

```
$ rsync -options source_folder destination_folder
```

Let us consider that you want to copy from `/home/student/data_folder` to your mounted USB pen drive `/media/usb_drive/data_folder`. Then, the backup command would be:

For CentOS or Red Hat:

```
$ sudo rsync -a /home/student/test
/run/media/student/name_of_drive/test
```

For Debian or Ubuntu:

```
$ sudo rsync -a /home/student/test /media/student/ name_of_drive /test
```

The preceding command will copy a test folder to your mounted USB pen drive. Of course, you will need to check the exact path for the mounted pen drive. As per the volume label of the pen drive, the exact path of the destination folder may change. We have used the `-r` option from recursively copying folder with all of its subfolders and files.

If we want to ensure that in the source folder, a certain file or folder is deleted, then corresponding files or folders should be deleted from the destination backup folder as well, and for that we need to use the -delete option.

If we want to backup symbolic link files along with ownership, file permissions, and time stamps, then we should use option -a.

Then, the updated command would be:

For CentOS or Red Hat:

```
$ sudo rsync -a -delete /home/student/test
/run/media/student/ganesh/test
```

For Debian or Ubuntu:

```
$ sudo rsync -a -delete /home/student/test  /media/student/ganesh/test
```

If want to observe the progress of the backup, then add the -v option.

For CentOS or Red Hat:

```
$ sudo rsync -av -delete  /home/student/test
/run/media/student/ganesh/test
```

For Debian or Ubuntu:

```
$ sudo rsync -av -delete /home/student/test  /media/student/ganesh/test
```

If file sizes are very big and you want to compress the files and then take a backup, then simply add the -z option. This will save network bandwidth if you are going to transfer GB-or TB-sized data.

For CentOS or Red Hat:

```
$ sudo rsync -avz -delete /home/student/test
/run/media/student/ganesh/test
```

For Debian or Ubuntu:

```
$ sudo rsync -avz -delete /home/student/test /media/student/ganesh/test
```

By default, `rsync` deletes any partially transferred files if the backup operation is interrupted. If we want to keep partially transferred files, then we need to add the `-P` option. The updated backup command will be as follows:

For CentOS or Red Hat:

```
$ sudo rsync -avzP -delete /home/student/test
/run/media/student/ganesh/test
```

For Debian or Ubuntu:

```
$ sudo rsync -avzP -delete /home/student/test
/media/student/ganesh/test
```

Backup across the network

For taking backup across the network, we will need to install the `ssh` protocol package. Normally, it will already be installed. If it is not installed, then use the following command:

For CentOS or Red Hat

```
# sudo yum install ssh
```

For Debian or Ubuntu:

```
# sudo apt-get install ssh
```

The command to synchronize data from across the network to your local folder will be as follows:

```
$ rsync -avzP --delete -e ssh user@ip_address:source-folder
/destination-folder
```

Look at the following example:

```
$ rsync -avzP --delete -e ssh student@192.168.10.55:
/home/student/data-folder /home/student/data-folder
```

If we want to synchronize local folders to a remote computer, then the command would be as follows:

```
$ rsync -avzP --delete -e ssh source-folder
user@ip_address:destination-folder
```

The actual command would be as follows:

```
$ rsync -avzP --delete -e ssh /home/student/data-folder
                   student@192.168.10.55:/home/student/data-folder
```

You will need to replace the username and IP address of the destination PC with the required username and password.

If the remote PC has been configured with port forwarding, such as when we have to use port number 12345 while using the ssh command, then the rsync command will be as follows:

```
$ rsync -avzP --delete -e 'ssh -p 12345' student@192.168.10.55:
/home/student/data-folder /home/student/data-folder
```

Automating backup activity

If you want to automate taking backup activity every day at 7.30 pm, then you will need to use the crontab functionality. We have already studied this utility in Chapter 2, *Drilling Deep into Process Management, Job control, and Automation.*

You will need to enter the crontab -e command and enter the rsync command in it.

For regular backup at 7.30 pm every day, enter the following line in the crontab editor:

```
30 19 * * * rsync -avz -delete /home/student/data-folder
/media/usb_drive/data-folder
```

The preceding command will back up data at 30 minutes past 19 hours or 7 pm every day.

I suggest you keep one backup of important data locally and one copy remotely. Local copy backup should be undertaken more frequently, and remote backup less frequently. Of course, you will need to decide backup frequency according to the importance of the data and your business requirements.

Embedding other language codes or scripts in Bash shell scripts

There is a way to embed other language scripts or code in Bash Script. In this section, you will learn about it.

Embedding other language code in Bash shell script

We may need to include other language scripts in Bash for certain reasons such as the fact that a certain complex task is already coded in another language. For example, storing the values for `pi`; other languages could be better at getting the precise value of pi due to their library functions. Let us assume that the user knows Lua language scripting. Then, embedding Lua language script in Bash would be undertaken as follows:

```
$ export PI=$(lua -e "print(string.format('%f', math.pi))")
```

The preceding line will inform Bash to save the output of Lua code in variable `PI`. In this example, the `-e` option to Lua informs Lua interpreter to execute next code. The Lua code will be enclosed in quotes.

The procedure to embed other language code is to call that language command itself, followed by the `-c` or `-e` options. We will study the `-c` and `-e` options later on in this section.

In certain cases, such as Python, we may need to type version of python as well, for example, Python (for Python 2.x version) or Python 3 (for Python 3.x version).

Please ensure that the embedding of other languages code should only be done if it is really necessary. Bash cannot do the certain tasks efficiently, but other languages can do it better way such as complex mathematical calculations and plotting of graphs using python. Every language has certain good points as well as limitations.

The syntax to embed other language code is similar for all languages. The parameter passed will only differentiate between `-c` or `-e`, depending on a particular language. At the end of this chapter, a summary is given. You may refer to the table for finding an option for embedding language of your choice.

While embedding other languages, we must take care about escape characters, which will be read by Bash scripts. The following example is to be avoided:

```
perl -e 'print "Hello I am Perl Script.n" '
```

In the preceding code line, `.n` will be interpreted differently by Bash than expected. We should make it as `.n`. Then, Bash will interpret it correctly as we have escaped n properly.

The updated code will be seen as follows:

```
perl -e "print "Hello I am PerlScript.n""
```

While embedding other language code, we should take care of quotes, backslashes, dollar signs, and a few other characters.

Sending output to Bash Script

There are many ways to send or receive data from embedded code. Other language-embedded code can send data to Bash using piping, saving, writing, or printing. Other language-embedded code can receive data through variables, files, user input, or pipes.

The following is an example of other language code sending output to Bash using pipe:

```
ksh -c "ls" | cat > ./save_to_file
```

In the preceding command, `ksh` is sending directory content to bash by pipe, which will be stored in the file.

We can eliminate the use of pipe from the preceding example as follows:

```
ksh -c "ls" > ./save_to_file
```

As we have eliminated the use of pipe, the preceding command has become more efficient. It is better to eliminate the middleman if possible.

Storing other language output to Bash variable

To save the output of other language code in Bash, the example is as follows:

```
$ result=$(python3 -c "print(10+15)")
```

In the preceding example code, we have embedded `python3` code in bash shell. The output of the print command which addition of two numbers will be stored in a `bash` variable result.

If we want to print the output of embedded language code directly on screen, then the example code is as follows:

```
$ python3 -c "print(Hello World)"
```

Sending data to an embedded language code

If we want to send data to the embedded language script, then one way is to send it via variable content. Look at the following example:

```
$ export location="/etc"; ksh -c "ls $location"
```

In the preceding example, we are initializing a variable location with the path or folder name. When shell executes the ksh command, it will pass path as content of $location. Then, ksh will print the content of the directory required.

Using data from file by embedded language

If we want the embedded language to open a file and use its contents for further processing, then follow this example. We have used the python3 way of opening and reading the contents of a file:

```
$ python3 -c "import sys, io; DATA = open('/home/student/sample.txt',
'r').read()" | sed -e "s|Hello|Bye|g" | less
```

In the preceding command-line code, the python3 command is opening and reading contents of a file. Then, it sends the content to the file to bash shell command sed by pipe. Sed replaces text Hello from file to Bye, and finally, it is displayed on screen by the less command.

Sending user input to the embedded code

If we want to send user-entered keyboard data directly to embedded code, then we should use the embedded language input-related command:

```
$ ksh -c "read INPUT; echo "You_typed_'$INPUT'""
```

This would allow the code to accept input from users. It waits for a user to type and hit *Enter*. After pressing *Enter*, this line would prints You_typed_Hello there.

Embedding Python code in Bash shell Script

Nowadays, Python is a popular scripting language, especially in data science and automation. You can integrate Python code very easily in bash scripts. We have used here doc for this purpose.

Let's write the shell script embed_01.sh as follows:

```
#!/bin/bash
function now_date_time
{
python - <<START
import datetime
value = datetime.datetime.now()
print (value)
START
}
now_date_time
Date_Time=$(now_date_time)
echo "Date and time now = $Date_Time"
```

Let's test the program as follows:

```
$ chmod +x embed_01.sh
$ ./ embed_01.sh
```

The output is as follows:

```
2018-04-27 01:53:58.719905
Date and time now = 2018-04-27 01:53:58.770123
```

Let's see an example of using bash variables in embedded Python code.

Let's write the shell script embed_02.sh as follows:

```
#!/bin/bash
export price=100
 python - <<END
 import os
 print "price:", os.environ['price']
END
cost=200 python - <<END
 import os
 print "cost:", os.environ['cost']
END
```

Let's test the program as follows:

```
$ chmod +x embed_02.sh
$ ./ embed_02.sh
```

The output is as follows:

```
    price: 100
  cost: 200
```

Embedding Ruby code

You can run Ruby code from a bash shell script. In this case, you will have one bash script and a Ruby script. You can simply call the Ruby script from within the Bash shell script.

If you want to combine both scripts in one script, then we will need to use the << heredoc functionality of Bash shell.

Let's write the embed_03.sh script:

```
#!/usr/bin/env sh
 echo "This is bashScript!"
 /usr/bin/env rubyScript <<-EndOfRuby
 puts 'This is ruby!'
 EndOfRuby
```

Let's test the program:

```
$ chmod +x embed_03.sh
$ ./ embed_03.sh
```

The output is as follows:

```
    This is bashScript!
  This is rubyScript!
```

Embedding other language code in Bash – comparative study

Most of languages allow other code from languages in their code. However, there are certain advantages as well as disadvantages.

The advantages are as follows:

- More functionality and variety
- Efficient code (if properly used)
- Useful for programmers because they can implement or reuse algorithms or functionality from a different language. Different languages have `diff` strong points.

The disadvantages are as follows:

- Execution is slow (if implementation improperly)
- Programmers need to know many languages
- Different language tools need to be installed
- Code becomes fragmented, sometimes difficult to understand

A summary of commands for embedding other programming languages

A summary of the commands used for embedding various other programming languages is as follows:

Programming language	Command for embedding script or code
ash	ash -c ""
ruby	ruby -e ""
jruby	jruby -e ""
rubyjs	rubyjs -e ""
python	python -c ""
python3	python3 -c ""
jython	jython -c ""
cython	cython -c ""
perl	perl -e ""
csh	csh -c ""
tcsh	tcsh -c ""
mksh	mksh -c ""
ksh	ksh -c ""

```
zsh                zsh -c ""
dash               dash -c ""
coffee             coffee -e ""
lua                lua -e ""
scilab             scilab -e ""
```

Summary

In this chapter, you learned about taking local backups as well as across a network. You also learned about automating backups using crontab. You learned about embedding other languages in bash scripts, such as Python, Ruby, and Perl.

In the next chapter, you will learn how database administration can be done using shell scripting.

Database Administration Using Shell Scripts

15

In the previous chapter, you learned about taking backup of local as well as across the network. You also learned about embedding other languages in bash scripts, such as Python, Ruby, Pearl.

In this chapter, we will cover the following topics:

- Automating MySQL database administration using shell scripts
- Automating Oracle Database administration using shell scripts

Introduction to database administration

Databases are used in computer programs to store information that will be needed repeatedly, such as user's information in bank accounts, where all the data related to bank users is stored in databases. In this chapter, you will be learning how to automate two very popular databases—MySQL and Oracle. Nowadays, many graphical user interface programs are available for database administration, but when we want to automate administrative tasks, we need to use shell scripts.

Working with a MySQL Database

In this section, you will learn about automating MySQL database administration. Let's start with very basic activities, as discussed in the following topics.

Checking the version of MySQL database

We will initially start by checking which version of MySQL is installed. With this script, we will ensure that MySQL is properly installed and we are able to communicate with it with root privileges. This script will report us the database version of MySQL. It executes a SELECT VERSION() query to get the value of the database version. Let's create the script mysql_01.sh:

```
#!/bin/bash
mysql -u root -pTraining2@^ <<MY_QUERY
SELECT VERSION();
MY_QUERY
```

Save the program and execute it as follows:

```
$ chmod +x mysql_01.sh
$ ./mysql_01.sh
```

The output will be:

```
VERSION()
5.7.22
```

Creating a database

In this section, you will learn about a creating new database in MySQL. We are going to use this database throughout this chapter. Create the script mysql_02.sh to create the database:

```
#!/bin/bash
mysql -u root -pTraining2@^ <<MY_QUERY
create database testdb;
MY_QUERY
```

Now save the program and run it as follows:

```
$ chmod +x mysql_02.sh $ ./mysql_02.sh
```

Show databases

To see all of the databases, we are going to use the command `show databases`. Create the script `mysql_03.sh` to see all of the databases:

```
#!/bin/bash
mysql -u root -pTraining2@^ <<MY_QUERY
show databases;
MY_QUERY
```

Save the script and run it as follows:

```
$ chmod +x mysql_03.sh
$ ./mysql_03.sh
```

The output will be:

```
    Database
information_schema
mysql
performance_schema
sys
testdb
```

Creating a user

Next, you will learn about creating a new user using the `MySQL` command inside shell script. The `CREATE USER` command creates a new user and we set a password for the newly created user. The command `GRANT ALL ON` provides privileges to make changes to database by newly created user.

In the next script, we will create a user and we will also grant all of the privileges on the database. Let's create the script `mysql_04.sh` to create a user:

```
#!/bin/bash
mysql -u root -pTraining2@^ <<MY_QUERY
CREATE USER 'user1'@'localhost' IDENTIFIED BY 'Test623@!@!';
GRANT ALL ON testdb.* TO 'user1'@'localhost';
select user from mysql.user;
MY_QUERY
```

Save the script and run it as follows:

```
$ chmod +x mysql_04.sh
$ ./mysql_04.sh
```

The output will be:

```
user
mysql.session
mysql.sys
root
user1
```

If you want to grant the privileges on all of the databases, then you just have to put `*` on database name. Then, the Grant query will be as follows:

```
GRANT ALL ON *.* TO 'user1'@'localhost';
```

In the preceding program, we have created one user named as user1 and have granted privileges to user1 on our testdb database.

From now onward, we are going to use the testdb database. Therefore, we will add use testdb; query to every shell script.

Creating a table in MySQL

We have successfully created a database named testdb and a user named user1, and have also granted all of the privileges on the testdb database.

Now we will create a table. Create the script mysql_05.sh to list the table:

```
#!/bin/bash
mysql -u user1 -pTest623@!   <<MY_QUERY
use testdb;
show tables;
MY_QUERY
```

Now save the program and run it as follows:

```
$ chmod +x mysql_05.sh
$ ./mysql_05.sh
```

The preceding command will not show presence of any table, as we only just have created our database.

Now, we are going to create a table named `Authors`. Create the script `mysql_06.sh` to create a table named `Authors`:

```
#!/bin/bash
mysql -u user1 -pTest623@! <<MY_QUERY
use testdb;
CREATE TABLE Authors(Id INT PRIMARY KEY AUTO_INCREMENT, Name VARCHAR(25));
MY_QUERY
```

Now save the program and run it as follows:

```
$ chmod +x mysql_06.sh
$ ./mysql_06.sh
```

The output will be:

```
Tables_in_testdb
Authors
```

Now check whether your table has been created by executing the `mysql_05.sh` script:

```
$ ./mysql_05.sh
```

The output will be:

```
Tables_in_testdb
Authors
```

Inserting data into table

Now we will insert some data into our `Authors` table. We will use `insert into query` to insert the data. Create the script `7_insert_into_Authors.sh` to insert the data:

```
#!/bin/bash
mysql -u user1 -pTest623@! <<MY_QUERY
use testdb;
Insert into Authors(NAME)values('William Shakespeare');
Insert into Authors(NAME)values('Charles Dickens');
Insert into Authors(NAME)values('Jane Austen');
Insert into Authors(NAME)values('George Orwell');
Insert into Authors(NAME)values('Oscan Wilde');
MY_QUERY
```

Now save the program and run it as follows:

```
$ chmod +x mysql_07.sh
$ ./mysql_07.sh
```

After executing this script, records will have been successfully inserted. To check this you will need to use the command `select`.

Retrieving data from the table

To retrieve data from a table, we use the `select` statement. We can retrieve all of the records from the table, or we can retrieve a specific record using the `select` statement.

To retrieve all of the records from the table, we have to use * in the `select` statement. So, the query will be as follows:

```
select * from table_name;
```

Create the script `mysql_08.sh` to get all of the records from the table:

```
#!/bin/bash
mysql -u user1 -pTest623@! <<MY_QUERY
use testdb;
select * from Authors;
MY_QUERY
```

Now save the program and run it as follows:

```
$ chmod +x mysql_08.sh
$ ./mysql_08.sh
```

The output will be:

```
Id      Name
1       William Shakespeare
2       Charles Dickens
3       Jane Austen
4       George Orwell
5       Oscan Wilde
```

Updating data

If we want to modify or replace the content of any row of a table, then we need to use the UPDATE command. We can modify single or multiple fields of a table.

Create mysql_09.sh to update the name of specified Id:

```
#!/bin/bash
mysql -u user1 -pTest623@! <<MY_QUERY
use testdb;
UPDATE Authors SET Name = 'Mansi Joshi' WHERE Id = 1;
select * from Authors;
MY_QUERY
```

Now, save the program and run it as follows:

```
$ chmod +x mysql_09.sh
$ ./mysql_09.sh
```

The output will be:

```
Id    Name
1     Mansi Joshi
2     Charles Dickens
3     Jane Austen
4     George Orwell
5     Oscan Wilde
```

Deleting data

If the need arises to delete a row, or multiple rows of a table because the data has become obsolete, then we have to use the DELETE command. When we want to make large-scale deletions in a table, this command is very handy.

Now, create the script mysql_10.sh to delete the record:

```
#!/bin/bash
mysql -u user1 -pTest623@! <<MY_QUERY
use testdb;
DELETE FROM Authors WHERE Name = 'Mansi Joshi';
select * from Authors;
MY_QUERY
```

Now, save the program and run it as follows:

```
$ chmod +x mysql_10.sh
$ ./mysql_10.sh
```

The output will be:

```
Id      Name
2       Charles Dickens
3       Jane Austen
4       George Orwell
5       Oscan Wilde
```

Altering a table

If we want to modify a table's basic structure, such as, adding an extra column, then we need to use the `Alter` command. When we need to put more information related to table objective, using this command, we can add extra column. We can use this command to modify table as well as database also.

In the next script, we are going to alter the table. Create the script `mysql_11.sh` to alter the table definition:

```
#!/bin/bash
mysql -u user1 -pTest623@! <<MY_QUERY
use testdb;
ALTER TABLE Authors
ADD ADDRESS VARCHAR(25);
MY_QUERY
```

In this shell script, we have added a new field named ADDRESS using ALTER command.

Now save the program and run it as follows:

```
$ chmod +x mysql_11.sh
$ ./mysql_11.sh
```

Describing a table

If we need to know more about the overall information or query the execution plan of an entire table, we need to use the DESCRIBE command.

We will create the script `mysql_12.sh` to obtain the table structure:

```
#!/bin/bash
mysql -u user1 -pTest623@!  <<MY_QUERY
use testdb;
desc Authors;
MY_QUERY
```

Save the script and run it as follows:

```
$ chmod +x mysql_12.sh
$ ./mysql_12.sh
```

The output will be:

```
Field  Type   Null  Key   Default          Extra
Id     int(11)      NO    PRI   NULL   auto_increment
Name   varchar(25) YES    NULL
ADDRESS varchar(25)        YES   NULL
```

Drop the table

If we want to remove any particular table from a database, then we need to use the DROP TABLE command. This command will remove the table definition along with all related partition information.

Now we will create the script `mysql_13.sh` to drop the table:

```
#!/bin/bash
mysql -u user1 -pTest623@! <<MY_QUERY
use testdb;
DROP TABLE Authors;
MY_QUERY
```

Save the program and run it as follows:

```
$ chmod +x mysql_13.sh
$ ./mysql_13.sh
```

After executing this script, your table will have been deleted. To check whether your table has been deleted, run this same script again, and you will get the following error message:

```
ERROR 1051 (42S02) at line 3: Unknown table 'testdb.Authors'
```

This means that your table has successfully been deleted.

Drop the database

If you want to delete the database itself, then the DROP DATABASE command will delete the complete database along with all of the tables inside it.

Now, we will create the script mysql_14.sh to drop the database:

```
#!/bin/bash
mysql -u user1 -pTest623@! <<MY_QUERY
DROP DATABASE testdb;
MY_QUERY
```

Now, save the program and run it as follows:

```
$ chmod +x mysql_14.sh
$ ./mysql_14.sh
```

After executing this script, your database will have been deleted. To check this, run this same script again, and you will get the following error message:

```
ERROR 1008 (HY000) at line 2: Can't drop database 'testdb'; database
doesn't exist
```

Working with Oracle Database

Oracle is one of the most widely used databases. In this section, you will learn about automating Oracle Database administration. Let's start with very basic activities, as discussed in the following sections.

Switching to an Oracle user

First, run the following command to log in as an oracle user:

```
$ su - oracle
```

In this case, the user was a student and after running this command, the user will be oracle.

Now, log in to your Oracle Database by running the following command:

$ sqlplus sys as sysdba

Enter the password you set earlier when installing Oracle. After the successful execution of this command, you will get the SQL> prompt:

```
[oracle@localhost work]$ sqlplus sys as sysdba

SQL*Plus: Release 11.2.0.1.0 Production on Mon Apr 30 12:02:53 2018

Copyright (c) 1982, 2009, Oracle.  All rights reserved.

Enter password:
Connected to an idle instance.

SQL>
```

Creating a user in Oracle SQL command line

To create a new user account in Oracle, issue the CREATEUSER command. We are going to create a user in Sqlplus command line, and we will use this user in all of our shell scripts.

To create a user, run the following command:

SQL> create user user1 identified by Test123;

You will get the following output:

User created.

The Grant statement

We can provide the newly created user with privileges by using the GRANT command. GRANT is a very powerful command with many options. It will provide privileges to user while accessing database:

```
SQL> grant connect, resource to user1;

You will get the following output:
   Grant succeeded.
```

The Define command

We can use the DEFINE command to create user-specific variables or we can modify predefined variables. This command assigns a CHAR value to the specified variable. It can assign a value to single or multiple variables.

Predefined variables

During the installation of SQL*Plus, eight variables are created and initialized. We will refer to them as predefined variables.

Variables	Description
_CONNECT_IDENTIFIER	Identifier of connection if available.
_DATE	Current date
_EDITOR	Information of editor used by EDIT command.
_O_RELEASE	Detailed release number of Oracle Database.
_O_VERSION	Version of installed Oracle database.
_PRIVILEGE	Current users privilege level
_SQLPLUS_RELEASE	Details of installed SQL*Plus component.
_USER	Name of the user

Let's create the script oracle_01.sh to get information about the predefined variables:

```
#!/bin/bash

sqlplus user1/Test123 <<MY_QUERY
define
MY_QUERY

Save the script and run as follows:
[oracle@localhost work]$ chmod +x oracle_01.sh
[oracle@localhost work]$ ./oracle_01.sh
```

The output will be:

```
[oracle@localhost work]$ ./oracle_01.sh

SQL*Plus: Release 11.2.0.1.0 Production on Mon Apr 30 17:19:29 2018

Copyright (c) 1982, 2009, Oracle.  All rights reserved.
```

```
Connected to:
Oracle Database 11g Enterprise Edition Release 11.2.0.1.0 - 64bit
Production
With the Partitioning, OLAP, Data Mining and Real Application Testing
options

SQL> SQL> DEFINE _DATE              = "30-APR-18" (CHAR)
DEFINE _CONNECT_IDENTIFIER = "orcl" (CHAR)
DEFINE _USER             = "USER1" (CHAR)
DEFINE _PRIVILEGE        = "" (CHAR)
DEFINE _SQLPLUS_RELEASE = "1102000100" (CHAR)
DEFINE _EDITOR           = "ed" (CHAR)
DEFINE _O_VERSION        = "Oracle Database 11g Enterprise Edition Release
11.2.0.1.0 - 64bit Production
With the Partitioning, OLAP, Data Mining and Real Application Testing
options" (CHAR)
DEFINE _O_RELEASE        = "1102000100" (CHAR)
```

Create user through a shell script

To create a new user, you must log in to SQL as a system user. To create a new user account, we are going to write the CREATEUSER command.

We grant all of the privileges to a user in the same script. Let's create the script oracle_02.sh to create a user and grant them privileges:

```
#!/bin/bash

sqlplus system/Training2 <<MY_QUERY
set serveroutput on;

create user demo_user identified by userdemo;
grant connect, resource to demo_user;

MY_QUERY
```

Save the script and run it as follows:

```
$ chmod +x oracle_02.sh
$ ./oracle_02.sh
```

The output will be:

```
SQL*Plus: Release 11.2.0.1.0 Production on Mon Apr 30 17:44:50 2018
Copyright (c) 1982, 2009, Oracle.  All rights reserved.
Connected to:
Oracle Database 11g Enterprise Edition Release 11.2.0.1.0 - 64bit
Production
With the Partitioning, OLAP, Data Mining and Real Application Testing
options
SQL> SQL> SQL>
User created.
SQL>
Grant succeeded.
SQL>
```

Creating a table

We have successfully created a user and granted them all of the privileges. Now we will create a table.

Create the script `oracle_03.sh` to create a table named `Writers`:

```
#!/bin/bash

sqlplus user1/Test123 <<MY_QUERY
set serveroutput on;
create table Writers(Id NUMBER(5) PRIMARY KEY, Name VARCHAR(25));
MY_QUERY
```

Save the script and run it as follows:

```
$ chmod +x oracle_03.sh
$ ./oracle_03.sh
```

The output will be:

```
SQL*Plus: Release 11.2.0.1.0 Production on Mon Apr 30 17:52:06 2018
Copyright (c) 1982, 2009, Oracle.  All rights reserved.
Connected to:
Oracle Database 11g Enterprise Edition Release 11.2.0.1.0 - 64bit
Production
With the Partitioning, OLAP, Data Mining and Real Application Testing
options
SQL> SQL>
Table created.
SQL>
```

Inserting the data into table

Now we will insert some data into our Writers table. We will be using insert into query to insert the data. Create a script oracle_04.sh to insert the data:

```bash
#!/bin/bash
sqlplus user1/Test123 <<MY_QUERY
set serveroutput on;
INSERT INTO Writers VALUES(101, 'ABCD');
INSERT INTO Writers VALUES(102, 'EFGH');
INSERT INTO Writers VALUES(103, 'IJKL');
INSERT INTO Writers VALUES(104, 'MNOP');
INSERT INTO Writers VALUES(105, 'WXYZ');
MY_QUERY
```

Save the script and run it as follows:

```
$ chmod +x oracle_04.sh
$ ./oracle_04.sh
```

The output will be:

```
SQL*Plus: Release 11.2.0.1.0 Production on Mon Apr 30 18:02:13 2018
Copyright (c) 1982, 2009, Oracle.  All rights reserved.
Connected to:
Oracle Database 11g Enterprise Edition Release 11.2.0.1.0 - 64bit
Production
With the Partitioning, OLAP, Data Mining and Real Application Testing
options
SQL> SQL>
1 row created.
SQL>
1 row created.
SQL>
1 row created.
SQL>
1 row created.
SQL>
1 row created.
SQL>
```

Retrieving data from a table

To retrieve data from a table, we use the `select` statement. We can retrieve all of the records from a table, or we can retrieve a specific record using `select` statement.

To retrieve all of the records from the table, we use `*` in the `select` statement. So the query will be as follows:

```
select * from table_name;
```

Create the script `oracle_05.sh` to get all of the records from the table:

```
#!/bin/bash

sqlplus user1/Test123 <<MY_QUERY
set serveroutput on;

select * from Writers;
MY_QUERY

Save the script and run as follows:
   $ chmod +x oracle_05.sh
   $ ./oracle_05.sh
```

The output will be:

```
SQL*Plus: Release 11.2.0.1.0 Production on Mon Apr 30 18:05:36 2018
Copyright (c) 1982, 2009, Oracle.  All rights reserved.
Connected to:
Oracle Database 11g Enterprise Edition Release 11.2.0.1.0 - 64bit
Production
With the Partitioning, OLAP, Data Mining and Real Application Testing
options
SQL> SQL> SQL>
     ID NAME
---------- ------------------------
    101 ABCD
    102 EFGH
    103 IJKL
    104 MNOP
    105 WXYZ
SQL>
```

Update the data

If we want to update a single field or many fields of a row from a particular table, then we need to use the UPDATE command. It can modify single or multiple fields at a time.

Create oracle_06.sh to update the name of the specified ID:

```
#!/bin/bash

sqlplus user1/Test123 <<MY_QUERY
set serveroutput on;
UPDATE Writers SET Name = 'demoname' WHERE Id = 101;
select * from Writers;

MY_QUERY
```

Save the script and run it as follows:

```
$ chmod +x oracle_06.sh
$ ./oracle_06.sh
```

The output will be:

```
SQL*Plus: Release 11.2.0.1.0 Production on Mon Apr 30 18:08:52 2018
Copyright (c) 1982, 2009, Oracle.  All rights reserved.
Connected to:
Oracle Database 11g Enterprise Edition Release 11.2.0.1.0 - 64bit
Production
With the Partitioning, OLAP, Data Mining and Real Application Testing
options
SQL> SQL> SQL>
1 row updated.
SQL> SQL>
      ID NAME
---------- --------------------------
     101 demoname
     102 EFGH
     103 IJKL
     104 MNOP
     105 WXYZ
SQL>
```

Delete the data

If we want to delete single or multiple rows from a table, then we need to use the DELETE command. We can delete single or multiple rows at a time. This is useful for deleting obsolete data.

Now, create the script oracle_07.sh to delete the record:

```
#!/bin/bash
sqlplus user1/Test123 <<MY_QUERY
set serveroutput on;
DELETE FROM Writers WHERE Name = 'demoname';
select * from Writers;
MY_QUERY
```

Save the script and run it as follows:

```
$ chmod +x oracle_07.sh
$ ./oracle_07.sh
```

The output will be:

```
SQL*Plus: Release 11.2.0.1.0 Production on Mon Apr 30 18:11:07 2018
Copyright (c) 1982, 2009, Oracle.  All rights reserved.
Connected to:
Oracle Database 11g Enterprise Edition Release 11.2.0.1.0 - 64bit
Production
With the Partitioning, OLAP, Data Mining and Real Application Testing
options
SQL> SQL> SQL>
1 row deleted.
SQL> SQL>
       ID NAME
---------- ------------------------
      102 EFGH
      103 IJKL
      104 MNOP
      105 WXYZ
SQL>
```

Drop the table

If we want to remove a table along with its definition, data, and partitions, then we need to use the DROP command. This command will delete complete table along with its data and partitions information.

Now we will create a script oracle_08.sh to drop the table:

```
#!/bin/bash

sqlplus user1/Test123 <<MY_QUERY
set serveroutput on;

drop table Writers;
select * from Writers;

MY_QUERY
```

After executing this script, your table gets deleted. We have written the select statement to check whether the table gets deleted or not.

Save the script and run it as follows:

```
$ chmod +x oracle_08.sh
$ ./oracle_08.sh
```

The output will be:

```
SQL*Plus: Release 11.2.0.1.0 Production on Mon Apr 30 18:15:53 2018
Copyright (c) 1982, 2009, Oracle.  All rights reserved.
Connected to:
Oracle Database 11g Enterprise Edition Release 11.2.0.1.0 - 64bit
Production
With the Partitioning, OLAP, Data Mining and Real Application Testing
options
SQL> SQL> SQL>
Table dropped.
SQL> select * from Writers
                 *
ERROR at line 1:
ORA-00942: table or view does not exist
SQL>
```

We get table or view does not exist error, which means our table has been deleted successfully.

Summary

In this chapter, you learned how to write and execute MySQL commands in a shell script, as well as how to write and execute Oracle commands in a shell script. Using what you have learned from this chapter, you will be able to automate frequently required database administration tasks.

Other Books You May Enjoy

If you enjoyed this book, you may be interested in these other books by Packt:

Mastering Bash
Giorgio Zarrelli

ISBN: 978-1-78439-687-9

- Understand Bash right from the basics and progress to an advanced level
- Customise your environment and automate system routine tasks
- Write structured scripts and create a command-line interface for your scripts
- Understand arrays, menus, and functions
- Securely execute remote commands using ssh
- Write Nagios plugins to automate your infrastructure checks
- Interact with web services, and a Slack notification script
- Find out how to execute subshells and take advantage of parallelism
- Explore inter-process communication and write your own daemon

Mastering Linux Shell Scripting - Second Edition
Mokhtar Ebrahim, Andrew Mallett

ISBN: 978-1-78899-055-4

- Make, execute, and debug your first Bash script
- Create interactive scripts that prompt for user input
- Foster menu structures for operators with little command-line experience
- Develop scripts that dynamically edit web configuration files to produce a new virtual host
- Write scripts that use AWK to search and reports on log files
- Draft effective scripts using functions as building blocks, reducing maintenance and build time
- Make informed choices by comparing different script languages such as Python with BASH

Leave a review - let other readers know what you think

Please share your thoughts on this book with others by leaving a review on the site that you bought it from. If you purchased the book from Amazon, please leave us an honest review on this book's Amazon page. This is vital so that other potential readers can see and use your unbiased opinion to make purchasing decisions, we can understand what our customers think about our products, and our authors can see your feedback on the title that they have worked with Packt to create. It will only take a few minutes of your time, but is valuable to other potential customers, our authors, and Packt. Thank you!

Index